Hidden BROOKLYN

KATELIJNE DE BACKER

INTRODUCTION

I live in Brooklyn. By choice.
– Truman Capote

Spread love, it's the Brooklyn way.
– The Notorious B.I.G.

That's my favorite place in the world, so far, that I've seen. I haven't travelled much, but I don't think I'll find anything to replace Brooklyn.
– Marilyn Monroe

Brooklyn is not the easiest place to grow up in, although I wouldn't change that experience for anything.
– Neil Diamond

Thank you for choosing this alternative guidebook about the mélange of cultures called Brooklyn. You will come to know it as a truly wonderful place and, in the end, a city of its own, filled with hope, possibility and excitement for the future. Like other cities with cool restaurants, hip boutiques, independent bookstores and so on, the coronavirus hit Brooklyn hard in 2020. But Brooklynites tend not to complain too much: they get on with things, they have tenacity, and they have soul, courage and beauty. True, some great places have closed and will be missed massively by locals and visitors alike, but then again, these challenging times also sparked creativity and entrepreneurship in Brooklyn, with many new delightful and exciting restaurants and shops seeing the light of day.

These gems, new and older ones alike, are what this book is about. It will steer you away from the obvious and the ordinary and take you off the beaten track instead, to explore places most tourists won't go. The focus is on Brooklyn's subdivisions, called neighborhoods, which all have a strong sense of local identity. Bedford-Stuyvesant is a historically Black middle-class neighborhood with close-knit block communities. Carroll Gardens and Cobble Hill are old Italian neighborhoods, and Brooklyn Heights is a celebrity-filled historical district. Park Slope is jokingly known as the home of lesbians and baby strollers, Williamsburg and Bushwick are the hoods of hipsters and artists, and so on.

Please keep in mind that this book doesn't cover everything there is to see in Brooklyn; no guide book could hope to do so. It is a highly personal and intimate selection of places the author would recommend to a friend. The aim is to inspire you to start exploring and to really get to know Brooklyn; we're pretty confident you'll fall in love with this borough, just like the author.

ABOUT THE AUTHOR

Katelijne De Backer has lived in Brooklyn for almost 20 years. She has worked at the intersection of business and culture her entire career. Born and raised in Belgium, Katelijne left for London in 1987, where she joined MTV Europe and developed and produced successful weekly alternative music shows. In 1997, she moved to New York City, where she became the Director of The Armory Show, still one of the most important modern and contemporary art fairs in the world. She has managed several other art fairs and was the Managing Director of the art gallery Lehmann Maupin.

Katelijne has always had a soft spot for big cities – first Brussels, then London, followed by New York. She moved from Manhattan's Upper West Side to Brooklyn in 2002 and she was immediately smitten with her new neighborhood of Brooklyn Heights. Her interest in music, art, food, design, books, films, has taken her to the most fascinating corners of New York City and Brooklyn in particular.

Katelijne would like to thank the many people who have helped her to create this book, and who stuck with her during the difficult time of the lockdown in 2020-2021. She's grateful to her parents, Greta Van den Broeck and Toon De Backer, to her sisters Chris and Els, and to the rest of her loving family in Belgium. Thank you An Diels for everything one could wish for in a friend; thanks Margaret Murray and Michael Blodget, the nicest neighborhood-friends; Emma Bruggeman and Björn Soenens, thank you for the many COVID-bubble dinners; and Jill Selsman, for being a wonderful explorer-partner-in-crime and a true New Yorker. Also, Katelijne wants to thank the many friends who gave suggestions on art, music, fashion, food, and much more, in particular Kristien Cornette, Trees Depuydt, Mathew Horsman, Johan Michielsens, Kim Mupangilaï, Beth Rogers Kral, Jendayi Small, Stephanie Theodore, Jelle Van Riet, Ventiko, and Robin Verheyen: thank you!

Of course, Katelijne would also like to thank photographer Gabriel Flores for his enthusiasm and for capturing the beauty of Brooklyn in his wonderful photos. Dettie Luyten for her guidance and for being the most patient publisher. The one and only Marc Didden for suggesting her as the author for this book. And finally, a big thank you goes out to Szymon Snoeck, the best son in the world, for his endless support, encouragement and love, and for writing the chapter on skateparks!

HOW TO USE THIS BOOK

This guide lists over 350 places to visit and things to do in Brooklyn, or things to know about the city, presented in different categories. Most of these are places to go to – restaurants, bars, shops, galleries, museums or streets and parks.

We have included practical information like the address, the phone number and the website where these are available. For the purpose of this guide Brooklyn has been divided into 8 areas (holding different neighborhoods) each with its own map that can be found at the beginning of the book. Each address is numbered from 1 to 358 and the area and map number are included in the description. This will help you to locate the address on the maps. A word of caution however: these maps are not always detailed enough to allow you to locate specific locations in the city. A good map can be obtained from any tourist information center or from most good hotels. Or the addresses can be located on a smartphone.

The author also wishes to emphasize that a lively place like Brooklyn constantly changes. So a delicious meal at a restaurant may not taste quite as good on the day you visit it. Ownership and staffing of an address may change and with it the quality of service and experience. This personal and subjective selection is based on the author's experience, at the time this guide was compiled. If you want to add a comment, suggest a correction, recommend a place or share your own secret place in Brooklyn with us then contact the editor at *info@lusterpublishing.com*, or get in touch on Instagram or Facebook *@500hiddensecrets*.

DISCOVER MORE ONLINE

Hidden Brooklyn is part of the internationally successful travel guide series called *The 500 Hidden Secrets*. The series covers over 40 destinations and includes city guides, regional guides and guides that focus on a specific theme.

Curious about the other destinations? Or looking for inspiration for your next city trip? Visit THE500HIDDENSECRETS.COM. Here you can order every guide from our online shop and find tons of interesting travel content.

Also, don't forget to follow us on Instagram or Facebook for dreamy travel photos and ideas, as well as up-to-date information. Our socials are the easiest way to get in touch with us: we love hearing from you and appreciate all feedback.

the500hiddensecrets

@500hiddensecrets   #500hiddensecrets

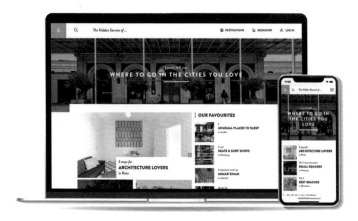

OVERVIEW

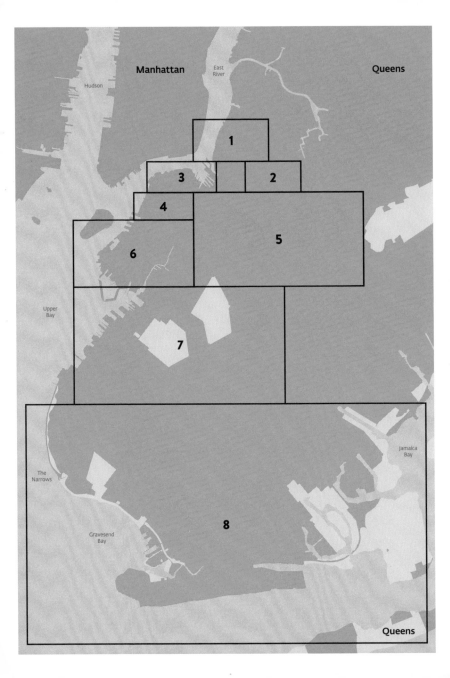

Map 1

GREENPOINT *and* WILLIAMSBURG

Transmitter Park

East River

Franklin St

John V. Lindsay East River Park

Avenue C

Marsha P. Johnson State Park

Kent Avenue

Wythe Avenue

Berry St.

Bedford Avenue

FDR Drive

Williamsburg Bridge

Domino Park

Metropolitan Avenue

Williamsburg

Corlears Hook

EAT — **DRINK** — SHOP — FASHION — **BUILDINGS** — DISCOVER — **CULTURE** — CHILDREN — SLEEP — **WEEKEND** — RANDOM

Map 2
EAST WILLIAMSBURG
and BUSHWICK

Grand st

Union Avenue

Morgan Avenue

Newtown Creek

298

60

40

247

249

Bushwick Avenue

Bogart St.

252

Sternberg Park

East Williamsburg

51   100 58

6 162

277

317

9

10

Broadway

Flushing Avenue

Bushwick

Bushwick Avenue

Myrtle Avenue

Broadway

East Williamsburg

Linden Hill
Methodist Cemetery

Flushing Avenue

27
132
35 274
47
76 248
44
113 10
Cypress Avenue
Maria
Hernandez
Park
Dekalb Avenue
Bushwick
163
Wilson Avenue
Myrtle Avenue
Gates Avenue
187
Bushwick Avenue

Map 3

BROOKLYN BRIDGE PARK, DUMBO, BROOKLYN HEIGHTS,

East River

Manhattan Bridge

Brooklyn Bridge

165

164

342

Main St Park

23

237

320

Dumbo

253

Plymouth St

269

258

120

251

Water St

265

25   301

28

319

343

119   142

234

Front St

70

307

175

Brooklyn Bridge Park

Brooklyn Queens Expressway

Manhattan Bridge

201

Pier 2

322

198

197

Trinity Park

Cadman Plaza W

Cadman Plaza Park

Whitman Park

Brooklyn Bridge

Pier 3

Brooklyn Queens Expressway

Brooklyn Heights

Tillary St

VINEGAR HILL *and*
BROOKLYN NAVY YARD

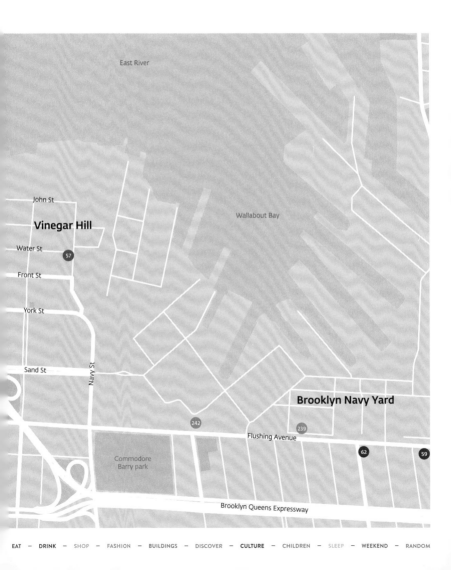

East River

Wallabout Bay

John St

Vinegar Hill

Water St 57

Front St

York St

Sand St

Navy St

Brooklyn Navy Yard

242

Flushing Avenue 239

62 59

Commodore
Barry park

Brooklyn Queens Expressway

Map 4

BROOKLYN BRIDGE PARK, BROOKLYN HEIGHTS,

DOWNTOWN BROOKLYN, COBBLE HILL, BOERUM HILL *and* FORT GREENE

Commodore Barry Park
297
271

Brooklyn Queens Expressway

Tillary St

Downtown Brooklyn

Jay St

Flatbush Avenue Extension

Myrtle Avenue

Ashland Place

315
71
190
54

Fort Greene Park
179

Fulton St

223

Dekalb Avenue

Livingston St

Fort Greene

Schermerhorn St

254
80
311
316

Fulton St

158
140
148
157
Atlantic Avenue

Nevins St

109
Lafayette Avenue
266
107
63

Boerum Hill

268
192
256

Map 5

CLINTON HILL,
PROSPECT HEIGHTS,

BEDFORD-STUYVESANT
and CROWN HEIGHTS

Dekalb Avenue

Lafayette Avenue

Jesse Owens Playground

Herbert Von King Park

199

Gates Avenue

Bushwick Avenue

Broadway

Gates Avenue

149

Marcus Garvey Boulevard

Lewis Avenue

Malcolm X Boulevard

Ralph Avenue

2

156

Halsey St

305

Bedford-Stuyvesant

Fulton St

146

Atlantic Avenue

291

St. John's Park

Utica Avenue

Ralph Avenue

Crown Heights

Eastern Parkway

Eastern Parkway

292

Lincoln Terrace / Arthur S. Somers Park

EAT — DRINK — SHOP — FASHION — BUILDINGS — DISCOVER — **CULTURE** — CHILDREN — SLEEP — WEEKEND — RANDOM

Map 6

GOVERNORS ISLAND, RED HOOK, COLUMBIA STREET WATERFRONT DISTRICT,

Governors Island

Columbia Street Waterfront District

Buttermilk Channel

Red Hook

Coffey Park

Red Hook Park

Red Hook Channel

Erie Basin

Van Brunt St

Columbia St

Columbia St

Brooklyn Queens E

Gowanus E

Beard St

Bay St

CARROLL GARDENS, GOWANUS *and* PARK SLOPE

Map 7

SUNSET PARK,
GREENWOOD HEIGHTS,

Red Hook Channel

Erie
Basin

Gowanus Bay

3rd Avenue

4th Aven

Prospect Expressw

20th St

**Greenwood
Heights**

220

Gowanus Expressway

4th Avenue

5th Avenue

218

218

Bay Ridge Channel

303

118

117

Bush Terminal
Piers Park

1st Avenue

Sunset Park

The Green-Wood
Cemetery

Gowanus Expressway

4th Avenue

5th Avenue

227

Sunset
Park

39th St

7th Avenue

Fort Hamilton Parkway

60th St

180

EAT — **DRINK** — SHOP — FASHION — BUILDINGS — DISCOVER — **CULTURE** — CHILDREN — SLEEP — WEEKEND — RANDOM

PARK SLOPE, WINDSOR TERRACE, PROSPECT LEFFERTS GARDENS, PROSPECT PARK *and* FLATBUSH

EAT — **DRINK** — SHOP — FASHION — BUILDINGS — DISCOVER — **CULTURE** — CHILDREN — SLEEP — WEEKEND — RANDOM

SHEEPSHEAD BAY, EAST FLATBUSH, MARINE PARK, BARREN ISLAND, CANARSIE *and* QUEENS

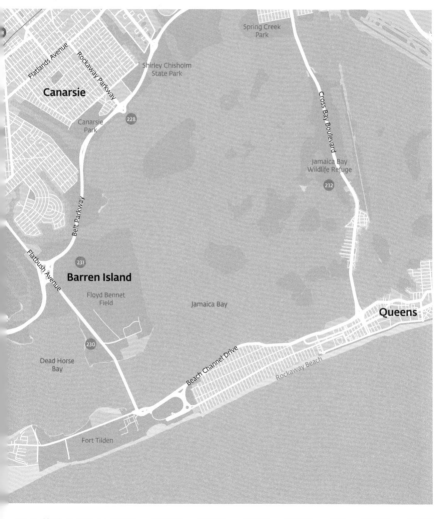

FISH MARKET
RAW BAR

GREENPOINT FISH MARKET

EAT 🍴

The best **P I Z Z A** comes from Brooklyn

1 **DI FARA**
   1424 Avenue J
   Midwood ⑧
   +1 718 258 1367
   difarapizzany.com

Let's start with a legend… 85-year-old Domenico DeMarco – or Dom as his friends call him – has been perfecting his renowned pizza since 1965. He still imports ingredients from Italy and cooks his pizzas every day, with a little help from some of his kids. Di Fara continues to be the No. 1 pizzeria in NYC for many. They have two other locations, Williamsburg and the Lower Eastside in Manhattan. Go check whether this Italian pizzaiolo still has that magic touch!

2 **CUTS & SLICES**
   93 Howard Avenue
   Bedford-
   Stuyvesant ⑤
   +1 718 552 2652
   cutsslices.com

Before Cuts & Slices, owner Randy Mclaren managed an expensive online sneaker concierge service which was worshiped by many NY rappers including Rihanna. He then came up with the concept of a pizzeria with high-quality, hand-tossed pies and a selection of the most imaginative, crazy toppings. Now Randy has a whole new following. He serves shrimp scampi pizza, chicken with waffles or French toast, oxtail slices, curry shrimp slices, jerk chicken, jerk shrimp, and much more.

3 L&B SPUMONI GARDENS

2725 86th St
Gravesend ⑧
+1 718 449 1230
spumonigardens.com

Gravesend in South Brooklyn is home to delicious and authentic Sicilian pizza and ice-cream spot L&B Spumoni Gardens. This charming place with its red picnic tables is always packed with local families and teenagers. It was founded by a southern Italian immigrant Ludovico Barbati in 1939. The pizzas are square, the ice cream is spumoni, a gelato with small bits of nuts and sometimes fruit mixed in. The dining room was redecorated during the pandemic, while service switched to the outdoor patio and deliveries.

4 LUCALI

575 Henry St
Carroll Gardens ⑥
+1 718 858 4086
lucalibrooklyn.com

This is how things used to go at this 15-year-old BYOB restaurant: show up before 5 pm, put your name on the list, go and have a drink, get a call when your table is ready. You then make your choice from the tiny menu of calzones and blistered thin-crust pies topped with cheese, pepperoni, and basil. Or at least that's how they used to do things here before 2020. During the pandemic, Carroll Gardens native Mark Iacono took phone reservations for outdoor dining for the first time. In mid-2021 he opened Baby Luc's, a slice shop two blocks away from the original Lucali.

5 PAULIE GEE'S

**60 Greenpoint
Avenue
Greenpoint ①
+1 347 987 3747**
pauliegee.com

The space is welcoming, romantic and easy-going.
The pies are trendy Neapolitan-ish, light and airy
with a deep char and a perfect crispiness. Try the
'Hellboy' with fresh mozzarella, Italian tomatoes,
Berkshire soppressata picante, Parmigiano Reggiano,
and Mike's Hot Honey. Or the 'Greenpointer' with
fresh mozzarella, baby arugula, olive oil, fresh
lemon juice, and shaved Parmigiano Reggiano.
They also offer a full selection of vegan pies made
with vegan mozzarella and vegan pepperoni.
Two blocks away, you can also check out retro
style Paulie Gee's Slice Shop with cool vintage
Coke signs.

6 ROBERTA'S

**261 Moore St
East Williams-
burg ②
+1 718 417 1118**
robertaspizza.com

This hipster magnet offers insanely good wood-
fired pizzas in a slightly ramshackle space, with
an industrial ski lodge look and feel, filled with
Mexican Christmas lights, picnic tables, and a large
pizza oven. The outdoor space has nearly twice as
much seating, its own tiki bar, and a sound system
that may play the Dead Kennedy's *California Uber
Alles*. A new location at Domino Park along the East
River opened at the end of the pandemic.

7 SPEEDY ROMEO

376 Classon
Avenue
Clinton Hill ⑤
+1 718 230 0061
speedyromeo.com

Speedy Romeo offers tasty steaks, chops, whole fish and burgers, but it's the perfectly charred pizzas that draw everyone to this old auto-body-shop-turned-restaurant in Clinton Hill. And with pizza names like 'The Saint Louie', 'The Dick Dale' and 'The Kind Brother' you can't go wrong. Should you not be able to make it to Brooklyn, they now also ship nationwide!

8 TOTONNO PIZZERIA NAPOLITANA

1524 Neptune
Avenue
Coney Island ⑧
+1 718 372 8606
*totonnos
coneyisland.com*

Take the F, Q or D train all the way to the end of the line and you will find a Coney Island treasure and authentic Brooklyn experience like no other. Totonno's, a 90+-year-old family-run business bringing you 'the best pizza in NYC!', serves up fabulous thin-crust coal-oven pizzas on paper plates with an old school Brooklyn attitude. This joint is cash only, just like in the good ol' days.

VEGAN *hotspots*

---

9 **AMITUOFO VEGAN CUISINE**
19 Bogart St
East Williams-
burg ②
+1 718 366 2288
amituofovegan.com

While plenty of restaurants offer vegetarian and vegan options in Brooklyn, there are surprisingly few full-on plant-based eateries. But at Amituofo it's all about sharing the passion for a vegan lifestyle. The menu is a mix of pan-Asian cuisine, from batter-fried king oyster mushrooms to General Tso's 'chicken', with a light touch of classic American fare, like the 'Beyond Burger'. All set in an elegant, bright and airy interior.

10 **BUNNA CAFE**
1084 Flushing
Avenue
Bushwick ②
+1 347 295 2227
bunnaethiopia.net

The lines outside Bunna Cafe after 8 pm may be longer than you would expect for a space that is both vegan and cash only, but locals who know the food will tell you it is all worth the wait. The plant-based dishes are filling, savory and perfect to share with friends. Ethiopian cuisine uses *injera*, the flat bread made from teff and barley flour, as a utensil. Don't miss the seasonal cocktails and traditional Ethiopian honey wine.

11 LITTLE CHOC APOTHECARY

141 Havemeyer St
Williamsburg ①
+1 718 963 0420
littlechoc.nyc

Little Choc Apothecary, NYC's first 100% vegan creperie, serves a wonderful selection of both sweet and savory gluten-free crêpes along with fresh pressed juices, smoothies, coffees, teas and baked goods. Former fashion model and owner Julia Kravets sources her ingredients from farms and distributors who focus on sustainability, with their local, organic, and fair-trade products. On the second floor there's an entire wall of loose teas from which guests can request personalized blends based on their health benefits or taste preferences.

12 MODERN LOVE

317 Union Avenue
Williamsburg ①
+1 929 298 0626
*modernlove
brooklyn.com*

Punk-rock vegan chef and author Isa Chandra Moskowitz opened Modern Love in 2016. The menu has plenty of vegan takes on classic comfort food from around the world inspired by Italian, Jewish, and Jamaican cuisines, all with a healthy dose of southern cooking to boot. The space is modern with high ceilings and industrial chandeliers. Some say it's a bit pricey, but if you're looking for classy vegan comfort food, it's the only way to go.

13 THE V-SPOT

156 5th Avenue
Park Slope ⑥
+1 718 928 8778
vspot.restaurant

This all-vegan, pan-Latino low-key cafe in the heart of Park Slope was founded by Columbian brothers Danny and Alex Carabaño. They serve dishes like a Colombian traditional plate of bandeja paisa, buffalo wings, and burrito carne molida, as well as Jamaican-style empanadas and *Carabaño arepas* (in honor of the founding brothers), their amazing tacos. They now also have a V-Spot Express in the East Village.

14 XILONEN

905 Lorimer St
Williamsburg ⓘ
+1 929 272 0370
xilonen.earth

Xilonen, which opened during the pandemic, is an upscale plant-based Mexican restaurant by rock-star-chef Justin Bazdarich, the man behind Speedy Romeo and the Michelin-starred Oxomoco. Named after the Aztec goddess of young corn, Xilonen aims to convert carnivores by using intense Mexican flavors to enhance the vegetables with a menu that that is 75% vegan and 25% vegetarian.

11 LITTLE CHOC APOTHECARY

OYSTERS, FISH
and other SEAFOOD

---

15 GREENPOINT FISH MARKET

**114 Nassau Avenue
Greenpoint** ⓘ
+1 718 349 0400
greenpointfish.com

This endearing little fish place is a seafood store, wholesaler and restaurant all-in-one. They strive to supply the highest-quality sustainable domestic and wild caught seafood, to both the public and most demanding chefs in NYC. Sit at the counter and watch the chef prepare the freshest piece of fish just for you. They have an excellent oyster selection and the wine list is outstanding too.

15 GREENPOINT FISH MARKET

16 LIMAN

2710 Emmons
Avenue
Sheepshead Bay ⑧
+1 718 769 3322
limanrestaurant
ny.com

Liman, which means seaport in Turkish, serves authentic Turkish-Mediterranean dishes in a lovely setting on the waterfront in Sheepshead Bay. Yusuf Basusta, the charming owner who knows the majority of his guests by name, cooks delicious fresh fish and seafood in this marine, boat-shack-styled eatery. Go for a casual meal or a fancy night out. Just make sure to enjoy the beautiful views of the waterfront in the back of the restaurant.

17 SAINT JULIVERT FISHERIE

264 Clinton St
Brooklyn Heights ④
+1 347 987 3710
saintjulivertbk.com

During the pandemic, this lovely eatery with Spanish and Japanese-inspired dishes, creatively turned their charming spot into what they called a neighborhood *despensa*. But they opened up again and still serve mostly small-ish plates inspired by delicious seafood you'd find in coastal areas around the world, like fluke ceviche, whipped mackerel, shrimp tacos and espanadas de pescado. Inside you eat at high-top and bar seating, and there are some tables outside in front of the shop too.

18 PETITE CREVETTE

144 Union St
Columbia Street
Waterfront
District ⑥
+1 718 855 2632
petite-crevette.com

This tiny, cash-only, BYOB, local seafood gem is one of those rare neighborhood places full of character with a serious and dedicated following. The food is simple but consistently good, and the owner Neil Ganic has a rather formidable reputation. He has been known to throw a lobster at customers who question the freshness of his product. But his product, the freshest seafood, combined with Mr. Ganic's 40 years of award-winning skills as a chef, is still the reason why people flock to Petite Crevette.

19 RED HOOK LOBSTER POUND

284 Van Brunt St
Red Hook ⑥
+1 718 858 7650
redhooklobster.com

The outstanding lobster is the reason why diners return to the Red Hook Lobster Pound time and again. Each roll is served on an authentic New England, top split, buttered and toasted bun with a side of your choice. They also have lobster mac and cheese, and delicious New England clam chowder. No wonder Brooklyn residents travel from all over to experience the best lobster in the borough.

20 LITTLENECK

288 3rd Avenue
Gowanus ⑥
+1 718 522 1921
*littleneck
brooklyn.com*

Housed in a space which looks very similar to a fisherman's shack on Martha's Vineyard, Littleneck is a cute hangout just a stone's throw from the Gowanus Canal. They serve lobster rolls, a fabulous bicoastal oyster selection, the daily catch and a happy hour. Sit at the zinc-topped bar for brunch or dinner, or just for some fabulous cocktails.

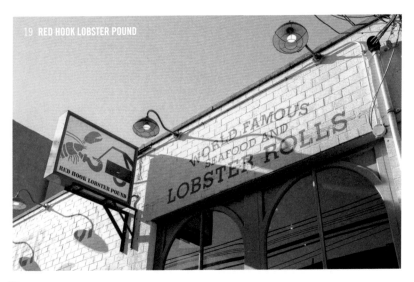

19 RED HOOK LOBSTER POUND

Eat with a fabulous **V I E W**

21 **ALMA**

187 Columbia St
Columbia Street
Waterfront
District ⑥
+1 718 643 5400
almabk.com

Alma is a three-story eatery that serves a diverse menu of authentic pan-regional Mexican cuisine and a vast selection of tequilas, mezcals and cocktails. Head to the roof deck – heated in winter – for brunch or dinner and enjoy the unrivaled panoramic views of Manhattan with sunsets that are pure magic year-round.

22 **BROOKLYN CRAB**

24 Reed St
Red Hook ⑥
+1 718 643 2722
brooklyncrab.com

A beach-themed tri-level indoor/outdoor restaurant that feels like sitting at a New England seafood shack. However, what you are staring at in the distance is the Statue of Liberty. Brooklyn Crab's menu includes numerous preparations of crab as well as fresh seafood. The restaurant doesn't take reservations, so you can make the wait more enjoyable with a game of minigolf downstairs. This place is more about the experience than it is about the food, but that's okay.

23 CELESTINE

1 John St
Dumbo ③
+1 718 522 5356
celestinebk.com

This upscale but unpretentious delicious restaurant, with floor-to-ceiling windows that slide open, offers magnificent views of the Manhattan skyline across the dazzling East River. The food is high quality and authentic, with a rotating menu of Mediterranean and Middle Eastern dishes. It's a great place to just hang out and watch the sun go down.

24 FORNINO

AT: PIER 6
Bridge Park Drive
Brooklyn Bridge
Park ④
+1 718 389 5300
(Greenpoint)
fornino.com

Make sure to arrive early – well before sunset – for the best spot on the roof terrace with the finest view of downtown Manhattan. Fornino's award winning pizzas with decadent toppings and perfectly done crusts, as well as their strong and tasty cocktails and sangrias, are what you are here for. Their other location is nestled in the historic Greenpoint district.

25 THE RIVER CAFÉ

1 Water St
Dumbo ③
+1 718 522 5200
rivercafe.com

This Michelin-star treasure, situated on a former coffee barge beneath the Brooklyn Bridge, is New York City's most romantic restaurant – period. With mesmerizing views of the East River and Lower Manhattan, an elegant atmosphere, and memorable food with an incredible wine list to match. Dom Salvador, the Brazilian pianist, has been playing jazz here for more than 40 years. The wine director, Joseph Delissio, had been on the job for almost as long when in September 2020 the New York Times announced that after 43 years, the sommelier had retired. This is the spot for a big budget binge. Just make sure to adhere to the dress code.

CHOCOLATES *from Brooklyn*

26 CACAO PRIETO
218 Conover St
Red Hook ⑥
+1 347 225 0130
cacaoprieto.com

Cacao Prieto is a beautiful chocolatier and distillery – don't miss the shining vats and pipes – with a retail space in front where you can buy chocolate, cacao-based liqueurs and rums. The founder is Daniel Prieto Preston, an inventor and aerospace engineer, whose family has been farming organic cacao in the Dominican Republic for more than 100 years. Their farm supplies all of the cacao for Cacao Prieto's chocolates and spirits. They sell chocolate bars in a variety of cocoa percentages and styles, and a line of bonbons in marvelous flavors.

27 FINE & RAW
70 Scott Avenue
East Williams-
burg ②
+1 718 366 3633
fineandraw.com

FINE & RAW is a true bean-to-bar factory, with an elegant coffee bar where you can have a glimpse of how everything is done. Everything starts with organic beans from sustainability-focused purveyors which are turned into finished chocolate bars, confections, and truffles. South African chocolate maker Daniel Sklaar uses innovative low-heat techniques – without dairy and using unrefined coconut sugar only – to preserve the chocolate's raw vitality and flavor. He also works with local artists and photographers for FINE & RAW's packaging, website and events.

28 JACQUES TORRES

66 Water St
Dumbo ③
+1 718 875 1269
mrchocolate.com

When French-born Jacques Torres opened his first chocolate store in Dumbo in 2000, he was the first artisan chocolatier to use cacao beans to make his own chocolate. He had the only chocolate factory in Brooklyn, and to this day his chocolate is still 100% made in Brooklyn. He serves bonbons, caramels, truffles, bars, cookies, ice cream, a delicious hot chocolate, and anything you can cover in chocolate. He has three other locations in Manhattan.

29 RAAKA

64 Seabring St
Red Hook ⑥
+1 855 255 3354
raakachocolate.com

Raaka makes chocolate that is uncommon both in terms of the process and flavor because it is 'virgin chocolate', meaning from unroasted cacao beans, to capture the brighter, bolder and fruitier flavor of cacao. Unfortunately, at the time of writing, the tours and chocolate making classes at the factory were on a hiatus due to COVID. They still produce chocolate however and the retail shop at the factory is open Saturdays and Sundays 12 to 4 pm. Orders for weekday curbside pick-up can also still be placed.

Let's talk **B U R G E R S**
and **H O T   D O G S**

30 **ALLSWELL**
   124 Bedford
   Avenue
   Williamsburg ⓘ
   +1 347 799 2743
   allswellnyc.com

This laidback Williamsburg tavern serves sustainably sourced food that is yummy, creative and always excellent. They offer four different burgers: the Classic Allswell Burger, the Portobello Burger, the Pioneer Burger, and the Cali Burger. All burgers come on a sesame bun with a variety of delicious trimmings, and all are fabulous.

31 **DINER**
   85 Broadway
   Williamsburg ⓘ
   +1 718 486 3077
   dinernyc.com

For more than twenty years this beautiful 90-year-old Pullman dining car, located on a corner under the Williamsburg Bridge, has been the place to go for excellent food and people-watching. But their amazing burger is the real star of the show. The charming waiters write out the daily menu onto your butcher-paper tablecloth, which is an entertaining touch. After all these years of being a quality hipster place, this place still continues to deliver the same quality of its early days.

32 NATHAN'S FAMOUS

1310 Surf Avenue
Coney Island ⑧
+1 718 333 2202
nathansfamous.com

Nathan's is an institution. The original Coney Island restaurant was founded in 1916 by the Polish immigrant Nathan Handwerker and is still in the same location on the corner of Surf and Stillwell Avenue. It is also home of the annual 4th of July Hot Dog Eating Contest. In 2021, Joey Chestnut set a new world record by eating 76 hot dogs and buns in 10 minutes. Eat that!

33 EMILY

919 Fulton St
Clinton Hill ⑤
+1 347 844 9588
pizzalovesemily.com

Emily is a small space with tons of character that makes very good thin crust pizza, but it's the Emily Burger that is the talk of the town. What makes this burger so good? Extremely high-quality meat, cooked medium rare in one big, juicy patty; plenty of melted cheddar cheese; sweet, caramelized onions; a brioche/pretzel bun; and a slightly spicy sauce. There's also a West Village location in Manhattan.

34 RED HOOK TAVERN

329 Van Brunt St
Red Hook ⑥
+1 917 966 6094
redhooktavern.com

This beautiful old space pays tribute to the working-class pubs of New York and classic American food on a quiet corner in Red Hook. A line of tables under electric gas lamps and stools with a white-oak bar, combined with the wallpaper and tin ceiling make this place look like real old New York. But the biggest attraction has to be its cheese-burger, which is a damn good New York City pub burger!

Must-eat restaurants for **FOODIES**

---

35 **FARO**

436 Jefferson St
Bushwick ②
+1 718 381 8201
farobk.com

This place is designed around seasonal vegetables, wood-fired dishes and exceptional housemade pastas, the heart and soul of FARO. They mill the organic flour for the pastas in-house. Located in the former sculpture storage space for MoMa, this one-Michelin-star restaurant has raised the culinary profile of Bushwick - unlike so many Bushwick hipster places – and feels like a place for grown-ups.

36 **HONEY BADGER**

67 Fenimore St
Prospect Lefferts
Gardens ⑦
+1 646 670 0601
honeybadgerbk.com

This avant-garde restaurant has a secret undisclosed menu that changes daily. It is run by a husband and wife who conjure unusual-looking food on tiny plates. The whole thing feels more like an art project than a restaurant. The open kitchen is the stage and the preparation of the food the performance. They call themselves a wild-to-table restaurant and source their produce from five sustainable local farms as well as their own bio-dynamic one. The menu is seasonal, organic and local (when possible) and offbeat. Go for an authentic experience and enjoy their tasting and Omakase menu in one of the cool private heated cabins.

37 ASKA

47 S 5th St
Williamsburg ①
+1 929 337 6792
askanyc.com

Swedish chef Fredrik Berselius spent most of his culinary career in NY, opening the first incarnation of Aska in 2012. This two-Michelin-star restaurant is now located in a former warehouse near the Williamsburg Bridge. It has a main dining room, garden and cellar bar, and serves excellent food that is inspired by nature. The service is warm and unpretentious. Eating here is an experience that you won't easily forget.

38 ALTA CALIDAD

552 Vanderbilt
Avenue
Prospect Heights ⑤
+1 718 622 1111
altacalidadbk.com

The food at Alta Calidad, chef Akhtar Nawab's restaurant, is innovative and playful. The son of Indian parents, he has a passion for Mexican food and makes dishes like grilled octopus, pork belly, and potatoes skewered over paella-styled rice. His tacos are filled with skate wing, seasoned with saffron, and garnished with crisp onions. The sun-drenched corner restaurant also has two outdoor patios.

39 OXALIS

791 Washington
Avenue
Prospect Heights ⑤
+1 347 627 8298
oxalisnyc.com

Just a short walk from the Brooklyn Museum, utterly charming and delicious Oxalis combines next level food provenance with French inspired preparation, serving perfect portions, flavors and textures in a mellow, super friendly atmosphere. From an unassuming exterior, you walk through the open kitchen, where you are greeted warmly by chefs and kitchen staff to a modern yet relaxed space, full of wood, steel and glass. Their attention to detail extends to their beautiful garden space replete with kitchen herbs and grape vines. You won't want to leave.

Dishes from
AROUND THE WORLD

40 **CASA ORA**
148 Meserole St
East Williams-
burg ②
+1 718 223 3116
casaoranyc.com

Casa Ora is one of the few upscale Venezuelan restaurants in the city; perhaps even the only one. Run by Venezuelan immigrants Isbelis Diaz (mother) and Ivo Diaz (son) and their all-Venezuelan kitchen staff, the restaurant aims to bring the beauty of Venezuelan cuisine to Williamsburg. The dishes they present are an upscale interpretation of traditional food from their home in Caracas. They kindly donate profits to families from Venezuela that are seeking asylum.

41 **OXOMOCO**
128 Greenpoint
Avenue
Greenpoint ①
+1 646 688 4180
oxomoconyc.com

Executive chef Justin Bazdarich shares his appreciation for Mexican food in this L.A.-style Mexican joint. The tacos and antojitos are the centerpieces here, with lamb barbacoa tacos, steak tartare tostadas and shrimp ceviche tostadas. The moles, salsas and soft, purple-hued masa tacos are all homemade, and there are plenty of tequila and mezcal drinks that make the entire experience eating there very festive and fun.

42 RANGOON

500 Prospect Place
Crown Heights ⑤
+1 917 442 0100
rangoon.nyc

Opening a restaurant during a pandemic is anything but evident but chef Myo Moe, who grew up in Myanmar (Burma) and who trained in Mercer Kitchen, took the leap. She and her husband had to close the dining room while it was still in soft-opening mode, but takeout and delivery kept Rangoon afloat. They paired with design firm Saw Earth to build a striking, well-ventilated outdoor dining structure. Order the salad of cold shrimp and mango in a lime-fish sauce vinaigrette, or try Moe's acclaimed bowlfuls of Burmese noodle soups, stews, and curries.

43 SOFREH

75 St Marks
Avenue
Prospect Heights ⑤
+1 646 798 1690
sofrehnyc.com

In a spare, modern dining room with an exposed beam ceiling, Iranian born Nasim Alikhani serves a bold, modern take on Persian cuisine. The food is authentic, well crafted, and delicious. Fresh-baked barbari bread, dried lime and herb beef stew; braised lamb with fava beans; and saffron and rose-water ice cream for dessert. Mouthwatering. The restaurant has an expansive sidewalk area in front and a comfy backyard area that is covered and heated.

44 TANOREEN

7523 3rd Avenue
Bay Ridge ⑧
+1 718 748 5600
tanoreen.com

Mother-daughter team Rawia and Jumana Bishara have been cooking delicious homestyle Palestinian and Middle Eastern food since 1998. Head to Bay Ridge and try their kafta tahini, baked ground lamb topped with tahini on a plate of rice with fried onions. Or dip your za'atar covered pita in the Eggplant Napoleon, a crispy breaded eggplant with baba ghanoush. Buy Rawia's cookbooks *Olives, Lemons & Za'atar* and *Levant*, which include many of the restaurant's recipes and take you on a culinary journey from Rawia's native Nazareth to her adopted Brooklyn.

45 YEMEN CAFÉ

176 Atlantic
Avenue
Cobble Hill ④
+1 718 834 9533
yemencafe.com

The Arab community with people from Lebanon, Palestine, Syria, Egypt, and Yemen, has made a lasting impact on the culture and eating habits of Atlantic Avenue. Yemen Café, with its authentic Yemeni food, stands out in this story. Start your meal with a delicious *Maraq*, a traditional lamb broth soup, then stick with lamb and try their most popular dish *Haneeth*, a slow-roasted lamb cooked in the Yemeni version of a tandoor oven. Another flavorsome option is the *Fahsa*, a traditional stew with pulled lamb which is served piping hot in a clay bowl with a warm flat bread. No alcohol is served at Yemen Café.

ASIAN *delights*

---

46 **DI AN DI**

68 Greenpoint
Avenue
Greenpoint ①
+1 718 576 3914
diandi.nyc

Chef Dennis Ngo's dishes are influenced by
Vietnam and Texas, and are incredibly tasty.
Di An Di is a very attractive place with lush
greenery, natural sunlight, a lot of pastel pink,
and Scandinavian-looking furniture. It is loud and
lively but incredibly tasty, and you won't have to
spend a crazy amount of money. Make sure
to check out the specials, you are going to want to
order those as well because they are, once more,
incredibly tasty.

47 **FALANSAI**

112 Harrison Place
East Williams-
burg ②
+1 718 381 0980
falansai.com

Eric Tran, a former chef at Blue Hill at Stone Barns,
took over a space that had been home to the
well-regarded Vietnamese restaurant Falansai for
the past seven years. Unfortunately, it closed due
to the pandemic. The new Vietnamese-American
restaurant is a continuation of the old Falansai but
Mr. Tran brought in an entirely new menu that
reflects his own ideas on this cuisine. He practices
whole animal butchery, meaning that he highlights
unique cuts of meat in a multitude of ways.

48 HAENYEO

239 5th Avenue
Park Slope ⑥
+1 718 213 2290
haenyeobk.com

According to Korean lore, *haenyeo* are the female free divers who collect shellfish from the depths of the ocean, and it is these strong women that are an ongoing theme in the restaurants of chef Jenny Kwak where she has been serving innovating Korean cuisine since 1992. In this place, everything is more or less perfect; very attentive and warm hospitality, a welcoming setting with plenty of outdoor seating and, most importantly, scrumptious food. Should there be a line, be patient and order a delicious cocktail at the bar, as the dishes at Haenyeo are worth waiting for. No wonder they have earned a Michelin Bib Gourmand two years in a row!

49 BIRDS OF A FEATHER

191 Grand St
Williamsburg ①
+1 718 969 6800
birdsofafeather
ny.com

Make sure to bring friends when you visit Birds of a Feather as the authentic Sichuanese dishes are for sharing. Co-owners Xian Zhang and Yiming Wang – who come from a finance back-ground and who also run the Michelin-starred Cafe China in midtown – opened this brightly lit space with a large wooden communal table in 2017. Birds of a Feather is the perfect spot if you want to eat delicious food without breaking the bank. The menu is varied, with many items under 20 bucks, and they have a no-tip policy. A word of caution: the dishes can be very hot, in every sense of the word!

50 HIBINO

333 Henry St
Cobble Hill ④
+1 718 260 8052
hibino-brooklyn.com

Hibino (Japanese for daily) is one of the city's best spots for quality, affordable sushi. The sushi plate on offer features seven pieces of the chef's choice sushi, plus your pick of a roll. Check the blackboard that waiters carry around as the menu changes daily. Don't miss the homemade creamy fresh tofu – served cold or warm – with grated ginger, scallions, and a soy-dashi sauce. It's truly delicious. Should there be a line at the door, just give your phone number and go have a drink at Henry Public a few doors down until they call you.

51 MOMO SUSHI SHACK

43 Bogart St
East Williams-
burg ②
+1 718 418 6666
momosushishack.com

The great atmosphere at Momo is typical of Brooklyn. Communal seating and a unique shack-like space give this eatery an exciting ambiance. Their specialties are unconventional sushi and Japanese tapas with an extensive list of vegetarian and vegan options. The signature dish is its 'Sushi Bombs', which are basically round pieces of nigiri sushi. The service is super friendly but can be slow at times.

52 UGLY BABY

407 Smith St
Carroll Gardens ⑥
+1 347 689 3075

Ugly Baby is just one room with just a few tables, murals in happy colors, and an even more upbeat guitar-pop soundtrack. It may be simple and affordable but chef Sirichai Sreparplarn's cuisine is all about novelty and powerful spice combinations, rather than familiarity. The spiciness is there to make things taste better, not to burn your mouth. At Ugly Baby you will probably find dishes unlike anything you've tasted in a NYC Thai restaurant before.

Oh so **CHARMING...**

---

53 **CONVIVIUM OSTERIA**

68 5th Avenue
Park Slope ⑥
+1 718 857 1833
convivium
osteria.com

Hidden behind the window of an ancient storefront, this traditional osteria feels like an Italian farmhouse that has been transported to Brooklyn's Park Slope. The authentic Mediterranean cuisine – Italian with a nod to Spain and Portugal – can be consumed in one of the two most romantic dining rooms, the patio outside, or in the rustic wine cellar full of old-world charm. Pastas and deserts are made in-house daily and produce is sourced from local organic farmers.

54 **GAGE & TOLLNER**

372 Fulton St
Downtown
Brooklyn ④
+1 347 689 3677
gageandtollner.com

The historic 19th-century Gage & Tollner originally opened in 1879. Three celebrated Brooklyn restaurateurs were hoping to reopen it on March 15, 2020, just when the city went into lockdown. After more than a year of pandemic limbo, the dining room finally opened a year late, but the landmarked interior was well worth the wait. Diners can now enjoy an array of classic seafood and meat dishes, as well as cocktails reminiscent of the 1940s in this magnificent space.

55 LILIA

567 Union Avenue
Williamsburg ①
+1 718 576 3095
lilianewyork.com

The space – once an auto body shop that has since been spruced up with handmade tiles and wooden banquettes – is huge, impressive and upscale. Missy Robbins, the chef who is an Obama family favorite, prepares simple fare from all over Italy, including wood-fired seafood, homemade pastas and classic Italian cocktails. The hospitality is warm, genuine and welcoming. The little Italian cafe to the side serves coffee, homemade pastries, focaccia and sandwiches for lunch, as well as aperitivo and snacks in the early evening.

56 RIVER DELI

32 Joralemon St
Brooklyn Heights ④
+1 718 254 9200
riverdeli
restaurant.com

On a quiet corner of the Flemish cobblestone streets of Brooklyn Heights, the cozy River Deli – run by a charming Italian couple – serves authentic Sardinian dishes inspired by their mother's and grandmother's recipes. River Deli opened in 2010, and serves fresh and delicious pastas, fish and seafood dishes, as well as classic cocktails with a Sardinian twist.

57 VINEGAR HILL HOUSE

72 Hudson Avenue
Vinegar Hill ③
+1 718 522 1018
vinegarhillhouse.com

Tucked away in the small, cobblestoned neighborhood on the waterfront right next to Dumbo you'll find Vinegar Hill House. This casual joint is the place to go for the cool vibe, the hearty homemade pasta, the fantastic wine list, the delicious sourdough bread, and the incredible pork chops. It's the consistently excellent food as well as the great outdoor dining that makes Vinegar Hill House one of the most wonderful restaurants in Brooklyn. Oh, and don't forget the Guinness chocolate cake with cream cheese frosting, it's simply to die for!

HOTEL DELMANO

DRINK 🍷

Where to get your CAWFEE

---

58 SEY COFFEE
**18 Grattan St
East Williams-
burg** ②
+1 347 871 1611
seycoffee.com

A sun-filled space with three skylights, a long attention-grabbing bar with lots of wood, concrete and plants. Named 'Best Coffee Shop' in America by Food & Wine, these coffee roasters make delicious coffee while supporting a sustainable business and taking care of their community. SEY is a gratuity-included operation, which means there is no tip jar.

59 BROOKLYN ROASTING COMPANY

200 Flushing Avenue Brooklyn Navy Yard ③
+1 718 858 5500
brooklyn roasting.com

At its peak, the Brooklyn Roasting Company had seven retail locations across NYC. Unfortunately, in October 2020, the company with its colorful logo that had been around since 2009, filed for bankruptcy. It's unclear what happened but in 2021 they opened a brand new space in Brooklyn's Navy Yard and, hopefully, will continue to serve their Fair Trade, Organic and Rainforest Alliance certified coffees in an unpretentious way to the colorful people of Brooklyn, where the company has its roots.

60 CITY OF SAINTS COFFEE ROASTERS

297 Meserole St East Williamsburg ②
+1 929 900 5282
cityofsaints coffee.com

City of Saints roasts its coffee in a gritty Bushwick warehouse and serves delicious espressos to local artists and neighborhood regulars at a small bar in the front. On offer are the basics – espresso, filter, regular coffee and cold brew on tap, plus a few tea options and a homemade soda. Small plates come from Doughnut Plant, Roberta's – the legendary pizza joint - and cookies from that great Bushwick bakery L'Imprimerie.

61 OSLO COFFEE ROASTERS

133 Roebling St Williamsburg ①
+1 718 782 0332
oslocoffee.com

An unassuming plain storefront with a simple blue-and-white sign brings you to a small space with happy and friendly staff who serve a large variety of delicious coffee and espresso-based drinks in addition to a good selection of pastries and treats – including some vegan and gluten free. There's not much space to hang out, so just grab your delicious goodies and go.

62 **PARLOR COFFEE**

11 Vanderbilt Avenue
Brooklyn Navy Yard ③
+1 917 966 6070
parlorcoffee.com

The carriage house of Parlor Coffee on the edge of the Brooklyn Navy Yard is open to the public only on Saturday and Sunday. They offer a takeout menu of espresso drinks, filter and iced coffees, a complete selection of their freshly roasted coffee, and home brewing gear. Go there to restock your supply or have a cup on the sidewalk out front. You'll find more outdoor seating right across the street in the Navy Yard. You can also enjoy Parlor Coffee from the cute battery-powered Blank Street coffee carts that are now spread out all over the city.

OLDEST BARS *in Brooklyn*

63 **BROOKLYN INN**
(1851)
148 Hoyt St
Boerum Hill ④
+1 718 522 2525

Located on a street corner in Boerum Hill surrounded by handsome brick townhouses, this historic watering hole was originally founded as the Boerum Hill Café in 1851 and is said to be the oldest still-operating saloon in Brooklyn. With its monumental carved-wood bar that was transplanted from Germany in the 1870s, this no-nonsense bar offers old-style camaraderie with plenty of draft beers to choose from. The cathedral-like façade and all-wood interior – with a touch of stained glass – has a very low-key vibe that transports you to an earlier era.

64 **FARRELL'S**
BAR & GRILL
(1933)
215 Prospect
Park West
Windsor Terrace ⑦
+1 718 788 8779

Windsor Terrace, the tiny area west of Prospect Park, is largely known for one reason only: this neighborhood is home to Farrell's Bar & Grill, one of Brooklyn's oldest drinking spots. Drinking at Farrell's is a quintessential Brooklyn tradition. This no-frills, cash-only joint with the coldest beer is one of the best places in the borough to celebrate St. Patrick's Day.

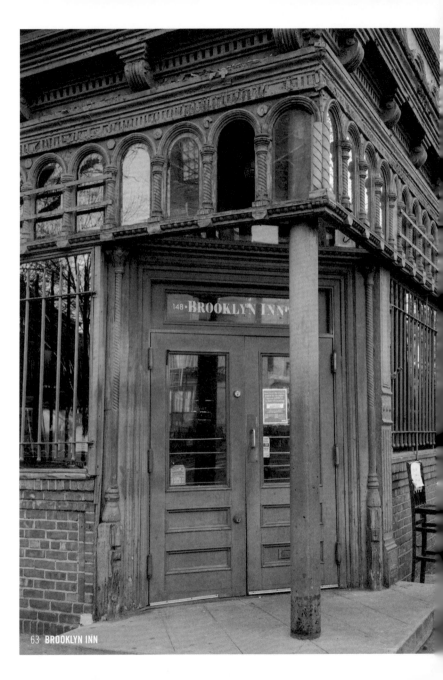

65 MONTERO BAR & GRILL
(1939)
73 Atlantic Avenue
Brooklyn Heights ④
+1 646 729 4129

Montero Bar & Grill opened as a union workers' bar in Brooklyn Heights in 1939. This cool dive bar, where lots of maritime tchotchkes line the taproom, is known for its rowdy karaoke nights. The bar had to close in March 2020 when the COVID-19 pandemic wreaked havoc on the city. After a 15-month closure, the famous vintage neon sign lit up again on May 28th, 2021.

66 SUNNY'S BAR
(1890)
253 Conover St
Red Hook ⑥
+1 718 625 8211
sunnysredhook.com

This small riverfront bar, that first opened near a railroad in 1890, was a popular spot for union workers to unwind after a long day of work at the nearby docks. It has since gone through various incarnations but has always remained one of Brooklyn's most iconic dive bars. Sunny Balzano, its legendary bar owner, passed away in 2016 at the age of 81. This tchotchke-filled spot is a wonderful meeting place for painters, writers, musicians, plumbers and locals. Try to catch some live music to experience its authentic soul.

67 TEDDY'S BAR & GRILL
(1887)
96 Berry St
Williamsburg ①
+1 718 384 9787
teddys.nyc

Teddy's initially opened as an Irish tavern in 1887 and has since changed owners a few times, with the latest handover in 2015. Classic details of this watering hole include an original stained-glass window with the words *Peter Doelger Extra Beer*, the original bar, tile flooring and woodwork. In addition to beer on tap, they also have a great food menu that includes lobster dishes on weekends.

68 **THREE JOLLY PIGEONS**
(1900)
6802 3rd Avenue
Bay Ridge ®
+1 718 745 9350

This institution has been serving Bay Ridge since the early 1900s, and is still an easy-going, welcoming place for a couple of drinks and maybe a game of a pool. The stained glass in the partition – originally used to separate men from the women –, the rich wood, the Gothic molding, as well as the locals who have been coming here for decades all make the place very unique. There's occasional live music on Saturday nights and cheerful karaoke on Fridays. Instead of happy hour, they just serve cheap drinks.

ROOFTOP BARS

69 **BAR BLONDEAU**
80 Wythe Avenue,
6th Fl.
Williamsburg ①
+1 718 460 8006
barblondeau.com

With sweeping views of Manhattan's skyline, Bar Blondeau is a playful, casual bar that opened in July 2021 atop the Wythe Hotel. The bar serves small plates and larger dishes for sharing, has a great natural wine list, and plenty of cocktails – classic, frozen, or non-alcoholic. One of the main attractions obviously is the view of Manhattan and the East River, and watching the sun set over Gotham from the outdoor terrace is always a thrilling experience.

70 **HARRIET'S ROOFTOP & LOUNGE**
60 Furman St
Brooklyn Heights ④
+1 347 696 2505
1hotels.com

This urban chic, lavish and modern rooftop is a popular spot among locals, hotel guests and tourists, with some of the best views any bar in the city can offer. Go for a cocktail during the magic hour before sunset to see the incredible panoramas of lower Manhattan, the East River and the Brooklyn Bridge, or wave at the Statue of Liberty from the reservation-only pool area. Just remember, all this luxury comes at a (hefty) price.

71 **KIMOTO ROOFTOP GARDEN LOUNGE**
228 Duffield St
Downtown
Brooklyn ④
+1 718 858 8940
kimotorooftop.com

Have a drink, smoke some hookah, eat Asian-inspired food and enjoy the views of Downtown Brooklyn while the DJ keeps the party vibe going. On the weekend there are three 3-hour timeslots: Brunch, Sunset and Nightlife, and a mandatory 10-dollar COVID charge per person. The dress code is elegant and fashionable so leave your yoga gear, hoodies and sweatpants at home.

72 **WESTLIGHT**
111 N 12th St,
22nd Fl.
Williamsburg ①
+1 718 307 7100
westlightnyc.com

The fancy rooftop bar on top of the even fancier William Vale hotel in Williamsburg is a great place to sip a cocktail and enjoy some of the best views in the entire city. They serve classic cocktails, rare spirits, craft beer and wine, as well as small plates with street food from around the world. The views from the bar inside are as impressive as the ones from the outside deck.

Brooklyn **BREWERIES**

73 **BROOKLYN BREWERY**

79 N 11th St
Williamsburg ①
+1 718 486 7422
brooklynbrewery.com

A very long time ago, Brooklyn was one of the largest brewing centers in the USA and home to more than 45 breweries. The Brooklyn Brewery, responsible for the popular Brooklyn Lager, was born with the idea of returning brewing to Brooklyn, and they have become a real institution. The brewery is open for indoor and outdoor service seven days a week with reservable small batch tours Monday through Friday, and free first-come-first-served tours on weekends.

74 **CONEY ISLAND BREWING COMPANY**

1904 Surf Avenue
Coney Island ⑧
+1 718 996 0019
coneyislandbeer.com

With lots of indoor space and many picnic tables on the outdoor patio, this Coney Island brewery was originally founded in 2007 but destroyed by Hurricane Sandy in 2012. A new brewery was built at the current location in 2015, just steps away from the original. They have several beers on tap, including Beach Beer – a crisp and refreshing ale, with a light body and a hint of citrus, some solid pub grub, as well as beers to go.

75 GRIMM ARTISANAL ALES

**990 Metropolitan
Avenue
East Williams-
burg** ⓘ
+1 718 564 9767
grimmales.com

While performing music in Belgium, husband
and wife team Lauren and Joe Grimm became
transfixed by the complexity of Belgian beers,
founding their Brooklyn-based brewery in 2013.
Their current location is huge with indoor and
outdoor seating. It feels family friendly in the
daytime and loungey at night. The artisanal beers
are unique and delicious and have beautiful and
colorful labels. Settling on just the one beer is
difficult, you will simply have to try them all!

75 GRIMM ARTISANAL ALES

76 KINGS COUNTY BREWERS COLLECTIVE

381 Troutman St
Bushwick ②
+1 929 409 5040
kcbcbeer.com

KCBC, the neighborhood's first brick-and-mortar brewery in more than 40 years, is located in a big open space with lots of light and plenty of seating just half a block from the L train. They offer a constantly changing menu of incredible sours, IPAs, and brew amazingly likeable pilsners and lagers. Make a reservation to avoid a wait.

77 OTHER HALF BREWING COMPANY

195 Centre St
Carroll Gardens ⑥
+ 1 212 564 6065
otherhalf
brewing.com

Founded in 2014, Other Half has a great tap list – the majority are IPAs – both on draft and in bottles, with fun names like 'Watching Grass Grow', 'Citra + Mosaic', 'Ideal Dream', and 'All Citrus Everything Oh2'. The space is industrial, the music good and dogs are welcome. Their other Brooklyn location is in Domino Park near the water, which is a great summer hangout.

78 STRONG ROPE BREWERY

574 President St
Gowanus ⑥
+1 929 337 8699
strongrope
brewery.com

This inventive brewery brews and serves hand-crafted beer in a garage-like space in Gowanus and at a waterfront taproom and brewery in Red Hook. They use 100% New York State ingredients for all their beers. Great service, chill vibe, and dog and child friendly... if they behave!

Where to sip your yummy
COCKTAILS

---

79 **CLOVER CLUB**
  210 Smith St
  Carroll Gardens ⑥
  +1 718 855 7939
  cloverclubny.com

Named after an influential group of Philadelphia journalists who used to drink, eat, and hang together in the late 1800s, Clover Club is a beautiful pre-Prohibition-style spot, where stylish waitstaff serve cocktails that will blow your mind. There's a democratic door policy – meaning no hassle to get in –, an atmosphere that is unpretentious, and a cozy back room with a fireplace. Occasionally they have jazz performances, and they do a killer family-friendly brunch too.

80 **GRAND ARMY**
  336 State St
  Boerum Hill ④
  +1 718 643 1503
  grandarmybar.com

Grand Army represents all the principles of a perfect neighborhood pub. The cocktails are prepared by co-owner Damon Boelte and bar director Kevin Baird and range from complicated creations to food-friendly drinks made to be sipped at the horseshoe-shaped oyster bar. Tuck into an abundance of crab legs, local oysters, and as many cocktail-sauced shrimps as you could ever eat. Grand Army has a timeless vibe that is a big plus in a rapidly changing Brooklyn.

81 HENRY PUBLIC

329 Henry St
Cobble Hill ④
+1 718 852 8630
henrypublic.com

Henry Public is a charming historic neighborhood pub with worn wood flooring, wall paneling, and saloon-style bar booths that serves solid burgers, a killer turkey leg sandwich, and marrow bones with toasts. The bartenders in the front of the house know how to whip up a classic cocktail, and in the back you'll find a semi-private wallpaper decorated dining room with an old brick fireplace and a darts board.

84 HOTEL DELMANO

82 PONYBOY

**632 Manhattan
Avenue
Greenpoint** ①
+1 347 441 4777
ponyboy.nyc

Located in a former piano bar, Ponyboy is a cocktail bar, funk club, restaurant and concert venue all in one. Plop down in the beautiful plush olive-green banquette seats, all part of a stunning interior design that was overseen by Belgian Kim Mupangilaï. Drink, mingle or dance to classic soul, disco and funk. They also occasionally host live performances by local funk bands.

83 THE LONG ISLAND BAR

**110 Atlantic
Avenue
Cobble Hill** ④
+1 718 625 8908
thelongislandbar.com

This classic art deco bar with an exterior neon sign that glows radiantly at the end of Atlantic Avenue near Brooklyn Bridge Park first opened in 1951 and was renovated and reopened in 2013. The wooden countertop of the bar features decades-old cigarette stains, and the lights over the old red-and-cream-colored high-back booth seats are intimate and old-timey. Cocktails are made by co-owner Toby Cecchini who invented the Cosmo at The Odeon in Manhattan many years ago. This easygoing yet stylish, smart but not pretentious place is one of the best hangouts in this neighborhood.

84 HOTEL DELMANO

**82 Berry St
Williamsburg** ①
+1 718 387 1945
hoteldelmano.com

Hotel Demano (no, it's not a hotel) is a beautiful space where you go for a great drink in a setting that's perfect for a quiet conversation. The inter-connected rooms combine to create a charming, intimate and discreet space, and the opulent chandeliers and old, smoky mirrors are authentic and very special. Slide into the leather banquettes or sit at the long upscale cocktail-centric marble bar for one of the best cocktails in this old New York tattoo parlor turned cocktail lounge.

85 SWEET POLLY

71 6th Avenue
Prospect Heights ⑤
+1 718 484 9600
sweetpollynyc.com

The shiny marble bar, the tufted leather couches and high-top tables, and the obligatory vintage-y touches like a tin foil ceiling and vintage desk lamps make Sweet Polly a super comfortable bar to hang. The service is impeccable, the cocktails yummy and strong, and the atmosphere definitely romantic. It is one of the more upscale drinking spots in this part of Brooklyn.

86 TOOKER ALLEY

793 Washington
Avenue
Prospect Heights ⑤
+1 347 955 4743
tookeralley.com

Tooker Alley is inspired by a Prohibition-era Chicago social-movement-cum-salon called Dil Pickle Club. Owner Del Pedro has been bartending in NY since the 1980s and is a pioneer in the cocktail revival. This comfortable, discreet, and quietly eccentric spot serves serious cocktails, jazz, humor, all in a much-loved bohemian style.

87 BAR BAYEUX

1066 Nostrand
Avenue
Prospect Lefferts
Gardens ⑦
+1 347 533 7845
barbayeux.com

Bar Bayeux is tucked away in Prospect Lefferts Gardens and is the go-to place for creative cocktails with funky names like Monk's Dream, Roaring 20's, Sazerac, Tin Tin Deo, and Damsel in Distress. They also serve old-world and natural wines as well as craft beer. They are mostly known for their excellent live jazz program, however. This dark, intimate spot has a beautiful wooden bar with walls painted a deep scarlet, and a garden at the rear which is open in the summer. No need to worry about expensive cover charges here. They have a one drink minimum per set, and generous donations are strongly encouraged. Absolutely worth it!

For **OENOPHILES**

88 BLACK MOUNTAIN WINE HOUSE

415 Union St
Gowanus ⑥
+1 718 522 4340
blkmtn
winehouse.com

The fireplace in the Black Mountain Wine House makes it feel like you are in someone's cabin on a mountain top far away from the hustle and bustle of New York City. The farmhouse bric-a-brac adds a cozy vibe, and there's a great neighborhood feel. Nearly every wine on offer is available by the glass, and the ones that aren't can be ordered by the half bottle.

89 COAST AND VALLEY

587 Manhattan
Avenue
Greenpoint ①
+1 917 838 7559
coastandvalley
wine.com

Should you wish to experience the laidback, easy breezy West Coast lifestyle in Brooklyn, then Coast and Valley is the place to go. The focus here is exclusively on wines that are produced on the West Coast, and the food is inspired by it as well. The place is bright and open, small but very charming, and they have a beautiful outdoor setup. The entire wine list is offered by the glass or bottle.

90 HAVE & MEYER

103 Havemeyer St
Williamsburg ①
+1 718 419 0722
haveandmeyer.com

If you're interested in exploring natural and biodynamic Italian wines, this is the place for you. If you are knowledgeable about natural and biodynamic wine and want to learn more about it, this is the place for you. If you're an all-out fan of biodynamic Italian wines and want to nerd out, then this is definitely the place for you. The staff's encyclopedic knowledge of their wines is legendary and they are eager to share the experience and joy of drinking them. The stemware is charmingly eclectic, the food delicious and the environment envelopes and transports you to a wonderful imaginary world.

91 JUNE

231 Court St
Cobble Hill ④
+1 917 909 0434
junebk.com

June is a lovely, endlessly romantic, intimate little place in Cobble Hill that specializes in natural wines. They have a huge, diverse wine list with plenty of affordable options, and the knowledgeable staff will happily help you decode it. The thoughtful, playful menu mostly focuses on small plates, and changes often. The curved banquettes, globe light fixtures and marble bar top make it all very vintage Paris. There's also a charming two-level patio and backyard.

92 **KING MOTHER**
1205 Cortelyou
Road
Flatbush ⑦
+1 718 287 0241
kingmotherbk.com

This Ditmas Park wine bar has a long wood bar on the right and a few matching wood tables along the left side of the room, and a cute outdoor space. Their natural, organic and biodynamic wines are all very tongue in cheek. Snacks include deviled eggs, olives, artisan cheese and the most delicious bread. Hot tip: join their monthly Wine Club!

93 **LALOU**
581 Vanderbilt
Avenue
Prospect Heights ⑤
+1 718 857 9463
laloubrooklyn.com

This narrow, white-walled spot is one of the best places for some low-key wine and snacks in Prospect Heights. They have a long list of natural wines, with a great selection of familiar names from famous regions in Italy and France, as well as lesser-known Eastern European options. Go and sit in the lovely backyard or, as Vanderbilt Ave is closed to traffic on weekends, eat out on the street.

94 **THE RED HOOK WINERY**
AT: PIER 41,
SUITE 325-A
175 Van Dyke St
Red Hook ⑥
+1 347 689 2432
redhookwinery.com

Located in a dock warehouse on the water, the stripped-bare tasting room indoor and the outdoor setting of this winery are equally beautiful. The grapes for the wines are picked from Finger Lakes and Long Island vineyards, but all the wine is produced from grape to bottle at Pier 41. Book a tasting to learn about the winery, how they operate, the history of Red Hook, and how to appreciate wine. And it all tastes even better with the amazing views of the Statue of Liberty and Manhattan across the East River.

95 **TAILFEATHER**
581 Myrtle Avenue
Clinton Hill ⑤
+1 347 240 5915
tailfeatherbar.com

This cute natural wine and craft beer bar – actually it's one big room with dark-gray walls and plenty of tables – has a little patio out front and a memorable, nice bathroom. The food is basic and fun, and some bottles of their wines are available at Tipsy, the neighborhood wine shop across the street.

96 **THE FOUR HORSEMEN**
295 Grand St
Williamsburg ①
+1 718 599 4900
fourhorsemenbk.com

The Four Horsemen, which is partly owned by James Murphy of LCD Soundsystem fame, earned a Michelin Star thanks to the culinary expertise and creativity of chef Nick Curtola. The decor is wonderfully minimal and the menu, which changes with the seasons, concise and succinct. The natural wine list is updated frequently. The sociable staff will happily walk you through the list and help you with the pairing. A great selection of wines by the half glass is perfect for abundant sampling.

Cool, **HIDDEN BARS**

---

97 **DYNACO**
**1112 Bedford
Avenue
Bedford-
Stuyvesant** ⑤

The windowless front room of Dynaco seems almost unreasonably dark, but once your eyes adjust you will notice the relaxed atmosphere that makes you feel like you are in a winter cabin in the middle of Brooklyn. The backyard fireplace keeps everyone warm and comfortable in the winter, adding a romantic vibe. They serve a terrific selection of classic cocktails and beers. The great music is never too loud. Make sure to enquire about the owner's wife homemade cake, and bring cash.

98 **LE BOUDOIR**
**135 Atlantic
Avenue
Brooklyn Heights** ④
+1 347 227 8337
boudoirbk.com

Below French restaurant Chez Moi you'll find this fabulous speakeasy, which is modeled after Marie Antoinette's own Boudoir in 18th-century Versailles. The decor is adorable with velvet walls, lots of pink, pictures of Marie Antoinette herself, and porcelain table stands shaped like ladies. The beautiful private room in the back features exposed brick from the old Atlantic Ave terminal. Cocktails are strong and tasty and come in fabulous stemware. Everything is reasonably priced.

99 LA MILAGROSA

149 Havemeyer St
Williamsburg ①
+1 718 599 1499

Tucked away behind an old laundromat you'll find a cool audiophile speakeasy where they serve mezcal, ceviche and good music. The mezcal is offered straight or in their riff on an Old Fashioned or a Negroni and served from behind a colorfully tiled bar top with religious candles and other traces of Mexican decor. Make sure to get in early or you might find it impossible to find a seat. Cash only.

100 PINE BOX ROCK SHOP

12 Grattan St
East Williams-
burg ②
+1 718 366 6311
pineboxrockshop.com

This dive bar in hip East Williamsburg/Bushwick has a fun theme, with friendly bartenders, and plenty of beer options ranging from cider to sour ales. They love dogs and have the best gender-neutral bathrooms with walls covered entirely with awesome collages made from 80s and 90s *Playboys* with lots of sparsely dressed pin-up girls!

101 THE HIDDEN PEARL

621 Manhattan
Avenue
Williamsburg ①
+1 718 383 3291
hiddenpearlbk.com

The Hidden Pearl is literally hidden behind a Japanese restaurant (Wanpaku), which gives it a cool speakeasy-esque feel. They serve delicious craft cocktails, beer, wine, sake and Japanese small plates. It's snug and intimate with a clean polished look, white walls, wood and gold accents. As it holds about 18 to 20 people, it's best to try and make reservations.

102 THE NARROWS

1037 Flushing Avenue
East Williams-burg ②

Tucked away in East-Williamsburg, near Bushwick, this art deco inspired lounge is the place to go for great cocktails, friendly staff and a cool ambiance. Given that it is rather 'narrow', it can get bumpy at times, especially when it gets crowded. But the cute back patio makes up for everything and is amazing in the summer. They have an oyster happy hour with 1-dollar oysters until 7 pm. Cash only.

103 WEATHER UP

589 Vanderbilt Avenue
Prospect Heights ⑤
+1 212 766 3202
(TriBeCa)
weatherupnyc.com

This tiny and cozy Prohibition-style cocktail lounge with white subway tiles and a bronze clad bar opened in 2008. There is no outside sign, which is why you may be forgiven for walking right past it. Just look for a door and push. The space is intimate and there's no natural light, but the bartenders know what they're doing; they are true mixologists and make killer cocktails. Try the Brooklyn (Rye, Dry Vermouth, Maraschino Bigallet China-China) or a house G & T. The really adventurous should request the 'Bartender's Choice'!

MCNALLY JACKSON

SHOP

Inspiring **BOOKSTORES**

104 ARCHESTRATUS BOOKS & FOODS

160 Huron St
Greenpoint ⑦
+1 718 349 7711
archestrat.us

Archestratus is an interesting spot where you can find a terrific selection of books on food – fiction and fact – as well as an array of specialty foods. During the pandemic they launched an online bookstore and added grocery items and fresh produce as well. Organic vegetables from nearby farms, Sicilian prepared foods, bread from She Wolf Bakery, coffee, tea, beer and wine. They provide information about virtual and in-person food events.

105 BOOKS ARE MAGIC

225 Smith St
Carroll Gardens ⑥
+1 718 246 2665
booksaremagic.net

The pink bookstore on a lovely corner in Cobble Hill is the brainchild of couple Emma Straub and Michael Fusco-Straub who wanted to share their passion for reading in an independent bookstore. The books on offer are new releases – including a staff curated selection – as well as the classics. The hidey-holes for children and books to read in them are fun. Their gumball-machine that dispenses poems for 0,25 dollar each is a hit with everyone.

106 COMMUNITY BOOKSTORE

143 7th Avenue
Park Slope ⑥
+1 718 783 3075
*community
bookstore.net*

This Park Slope institution is Brooklyn's oldest operating bookstore and opened in 1971. A cozy, dark-wood hideaway, this independent store has a solid collection of publications by smaller presses and emerging writers. Readings by Brooklyn authors and fellow customers – Paul Auster, Siri Hustvedt, Mary Morris, Jon Scieszka, etc. – draw a literature-loving crowd. The intelligent and friendly staff is keen to recommend titles for adults as well as for children. It's easy to see why so many locals find a good reason to spend the afternoon here or in the cute backyard, curled up with a novel.

107 GREENLIGHT BOOKSTORE

686 Fulton St
Fort Greene ④
+1 718 246 0200
*greenlight
bookstore.com*

Greenlight Bookstore in leafy Fort Greene was founded in 2009 by two women who were inspired by the idea of giving their neighborhood a literary sanctuary, and at the same time were passionate about supporting its community. This gem of a shop has big street-facing windows, a wide selection of new and old reads, as well as a very solid programming with weekly reading events and gatherings held in the large front room.

108 UNNAMEABLE BOOKS

600 Vanderbilt
Avenue
Prospect Heights ⑤
+1 718 789 1534
*unnameablebooks.
square.site*

This tiny, popular bookstore is chock-full of poetry, fiction, art books, comics, and all sorts of obscure titles. The store is well-organized, has an eclectic collection of used books and carries work from small independent presses. Readings, talks and book launches happen in the yard or in a basement space.

109 THE CENTER FOR FICTION

15 Lafayette Avenue
Fort Greene ④
+1 212 755 6710
centerforfiction.org

The stunning new home for The Center for Fiction – a nonprofit literary organization solely dedicated to celebrating fiction – opened in February 2019 and includes a bookstore, a cafe, a library, classrooms and a 160-seat auditorium. The spacious, sun-filled, three-story space is a peaceful site for both readers and writers. Founded in 1820 as The New York Mercantile Library, the Center was originally a lending library for mercantile workers. The current library features historic and rare finds as well as the latest acquisitions.

109 THE CENTER FOR FICTION

110 QUIMBY'S BOOKSTORE NYC

536 Metropolitan Avenue
Williamsburg ⓘ
quimbysnyc.com

Originally from Chicago, this beautiful and unusual gallery/bookstore opened its Williamsburg location in 2017. They specialize in zines, independently published and small press books, and one-of-a-kind artist-created gifts. In addition, they offer a wide selection of cards, prints, buttons, patches and stickers. As Quimby's NYC does not sell comics or graphic novels, you will need to go next-door to Desert Island Comics.

111 MCNALLY JACKSON

76 N 4th St, Unit G
Williamsburg ⓘ
+1 718 387 0115
mcnallyjackson.com

This high-end independent New York bookseller is easily one of the most stunning. With an open floor plan and high ceilings, its beautiful appearance is mesmerizing but it's the amazing variety of books that will have you returning. Literature from across the globe, books on everything from architecture and spirituality to travel and self-help, a section for kids, and an extensive magazine rack. In short, something to suit the tastes of every bookworm. The staff are usually busy but efficient; they leave you alone until you need them, and their recommendations are always great.

112 SPOONBILL & SUGARTOWN BOOKS

218 Bedford Avenue
Williamsburg ⓘ
+1 718 387 7322
spoonbillbooks.com

Brooklyn almost lost this iconic Williamsburg bookshop due to the coronavirus crisis, but a crowdfunding campaign saved the store. Spoonbill & Sugartown has served as a community space for readings and earned an international reputation for its eclectic range of new, secondhand and rare books on contemporary art, literature, philosophy and design.

113 **HUMAN RELATIONS**

1067 Flushing
Avenue
East Williams-
burg ②
*humanrelations
books.com*

Human Relations is a very well-organized used bookstore with a close following. The place is compact and filled with used and some new books on a wide range of subjects; philosophy, film noir, history, art, science, science fiction, food, drama and foreign language. Its layout is perfect for browsing, and the knowledgeable staff will give great recommendations for your next read.

114 **WORD**

126 Franklin St
Greenpoint ①
+1 718 383 0096
wordbookstores.com

Word, an independent, small bookshop owned by Christine Onorati and her husband Vincent, is filled with books for all tastes and ages. The well-curated selection of fiction, non-fiction, and graphic novels includes classics and contemporary authors. They also have a small children's area in the back, a stationery corner and a gorgeous selection of cookbooks. A fun bulletin board with literature-based classified ads for the NYC area can help you find the perfect roommate, start a new romance, or just find a new friend, all based on what they like to read.

Indoor and outdoor **MARKETS**

115 ARTISTS & FLEAS

70 N 7th St
Williamsburg ⓘ
+1 917 488 4203
artistsandfleas.com

Artists & Fleas markets are organized on the east and west coast of the USA, but the flagship one is in Williamsburg. It was established in 2003 in a former dry goods and provisions warehouse and is the meeting place for creators and buyers. This is one of the best spots to exhibit and discover what's new and exciting in fashion, vintage, art, design and more.

116 SMORGASBURG

90 Kent Avenue
Williamsburg ⓘ
smorgasburg.com

Smorgasburg is a popular open-air foodie market that attracts people from all over NYC to eat from over 100 local food vendors and to enjoy a full outdoor bar. It is organized on Saturdays in Williamsburg and Sundays in Prospect Park. The Williamsburg one is located in Marsha P. Johnson State Park on Williamsburg's waterfront with killer views of the Manhattan skyline.

117 FOOD HALL IN INDUSTRY CITY

220 36th St
Sunset Park ⓘ
+1 718 865 2729
industrycity.com

From Japanese to Mediterranean, burgers, tacos, to a brewery, Industry City's Food Hall is a yummy gourmet gathering place that has all the potential to become a great culinary micro city. You can find almost anything here, from hip German döner kebab to Korean comfort food. Discover many of the hip Brooklyn spots and Brooklyn-based purveyors all in one area.

118 JAPAN VILLAGE

934 3rd Avenue
Sunset Park ⑦
+1 347 584 4579
japanvillage.com

This massive food hall dedicated to all things Japanese brings together food stalls, an izakaya restaurant, and a grocery store. Fresh soba and udon noodles, a liquor store that stocks Japanese sake and whiskey, and the izakaya restaurant that offers grilled chicken skewers and sashimi. The Sunrise Mart has a varied selection of Japanese products, plus it comes with its own butcher's shop and tofu market.

121 TRADER JOE'S

121 TRADER JOE'S

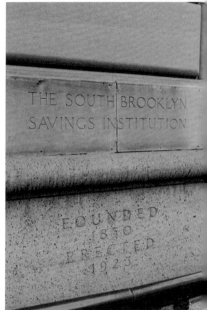

THE SOUTH BROOKLYN
SAVINGS INSTITUTION

FOUNDED
1850
ERECTED
1923

119 BROOKLYN FLEA

80 Pearl St
Dumbo ③
+1 718 928 6603
brooklynflea.com

Every weekend of the year there is a Brooklyn Flea somewhere in New York City. The one in Dumbo happens on Sundays and is not too big. Around fifty vendors of furniture, vintage clothing, collectibles and antiques, as well as a nicely curated mix of jewelry, art and crafts by local artisans and designers, plus delicious food come together in Pearl Street and under the Manhattan Bridge Archway. The other Brooklyn Flea happens on Saturdays in Williamsburg.

120 TIME OUT MARKET NEW YORK

55 Water St
Dumbo ③
+1 917 810 4855
timeoutmarket.com/
newyork

This waterfront food hall serves up eats and entertainment that is carefully selected by the staff of Time Out New York. It houses some of the better restaurants in the city under one roof. The scenic views of the Manhattan skyline, Brooklyn Bridge, Manhattan Bridge and quick access to the Brooklyn Bridge Park and Jane's Carousel are a plus.

121 TRADER JOE'S

130 Court St
Cobble Hill ④
+1 718 246 8460
traderjoes.com

There are 12 Trader Joe's in New York City, but the most beautiful one is in the converted bank building of The South Brooklyn Savings Institution on the corner of Court Street and Atlantic Avenue. The building opened as a bank in 1924, and Trader Joe's moved in 84 years later. Trader Joe's describes itself as 'your neighborhood grocery store', where 80% of the goods are sold under the Trader Joe's brand. Products include organic foods, vegetarian foods, unusual frozen foods, imported foods, and 'alternative' vegan and vegetarian options.

Some of the best **SPECIALTY FOOD STORES**

122 **ACME SMOKED FISH**

30 Gem St
Greenpoint ⓘ
+1 718 383 8585
acmesmokedfish.com

Harry Brownstein arrived in Brooklyn from Russia in 1906 and began selling the fish he bought from local smokehouses to stores out of a horse-drawn cart. Almost 50 years later in 1954, Harry and his two sons opened Acme at its current location on Gem Street. As a wholesaler, they pack and ship fish to markets and restaurants all over the USA, but what not everyone knows is that once a week, on Fish Friday, Acme opens its doors for a few hours to let locals buy their smoked salmon, pickled herring and whitefish salad directly from the source.

123 **HEATONIST**

121 Wythe Avenue
Williamsburg ⓘ
+1 718 599 0838
heatonist.com

In case you've never heard of a hot sauce sommelier, go visit Heatonist in Williamsburg and ask one for a complimentary guided tasting. The sauces are selected from over 100 varieties of small-batch, all-natural hot sauces curated by a team of makers from around the world. Some sauces are made locally in New York City and others are sourced from different parts of the country. Some sauces are sweet, tangy, and mild, and some are really hot or take longer to kick in. This unique destination is fun, and full of hot surprises.

124 BELLOCQ TEA ATELIER

104 West St
Greenpoint ⓘ
+1 800 495 5416
bellocqtea.com

You know you have arrived at Bellocq when you see a small black and white plaque on the front door, a rope-hung metal teapot, and a simple welcome sign somewhere in a quiet corner of Greenpoint. This tea atelier focuses exclusively on full leaf varieties and offers more than 50 pure teas. The shop is divided into two spaces. The front room has the entire collection of loose-leaf teas, tea accessories and books. In the back room you can sample the teas in the lounge. More recently, they added a collection of expertly crafted, perfumed candles inspired by the teas to the product range.

125 MONGER'S PALATE

192 Driggs Avenue
Greenpoint ⓘ
+1 718 383 0612
mongerspalate.com

Cheesemonger Lisa Griffin is an American Cheese Society Certified Professional who gained her experience at renowned Manhattan's Murray's Cheese. At Monger's Palate she brings a personalized cheese guide, old world staples, and American and international artisan cheeses. The shop also sells charcuterie and many accompaniments, from local honey to crackers. They also do pre-packed picnic baskets perfect for the park, beach or rooftop.

126 PAISANOS THE BUTCHER SHOP

162 Smith St
Boerum Hill ④
+1 718 855 2641
*paisanos
butchershop.com*

When you walk into this haven of all things Italian, you will discover an amazing selection of dry-aged steaks, house-made sausages and exotic meats, along with many other delicious food products. This old-school family-owned butcher's shop, which has been in business since 1960, combines quality products with great service and a dedicated following of loyal customers. Don't forget to ask for the Paisanos Sandwich, you won't be disappointed.

127 SAHADI'S

187 Atlantic
Avenue
Brooklyn Heights ④
+1 718 624 4550
sahadis.com

Originally from Lebanon, the Sahadi family established this Middle Eastern food bazaar in Manhattan in 1895 and moved to Atlantic Avenue in 1948. They now occupy three consecutive storefronts, and it is a true delight to walk through. First up is the bulk section with ancient grains and exquisite spices, bins of freshly roasted nuts, dried fruits, and imported olives, as well as old-fashioned barrels of coffee beans. Specialty cheeses, smoked fish, and pâtés fill up the refrigerators further back, but the deli at the rear is the ream revelation: hundreds of pounds of hummus produced daily, along with spinach pies, stuffed grape leaves, kibbeh, and much more. If you buy one thing at Sahadi's, let it be their hummus.

128 STEVE'S AUTHENTIC KEY LIME PIE

185 Van Dyke St
Red Hook ⑥
+1 718 858 5333
keylime.com

Located in an industrial building by the water, Steve's Authentic Key Lime Pie only sells... key lime pies. They have a classic ten-inch pie, a smaller eight-inch pie, the individual four-inch tart, and The Teaser, a three-inch mini-tart. They also offer a frozen-on-a-stick key lime pie dipped in chocolate Swingles. Steve's pies are authentic and made with 100% pure, freshly squeezed key lime juice. Eat your pie in the park next door and don't forget to enjoy the fantastic view of Manhattan.

The best **RECORD STORES**

in town

129 **CHARLIE'S CALYPSO CITY**

1273 Fulton St
Bedford-
Stuyvesant ⑤
+1 646 979 0125

Charlie's Calypso City is sandwiched between a phone store and a McDonald's in the heart of Bed-Stuy. The man behind the shop, here since 1972, is Rawlston Charles, an immigrant from Trinidad and Tobago. Charlie's Calypso City is a real hub for the Caribbean community and has become an essential part of the annual West Indian American Day Parade.

130 **BLACK GOLD RECORDS**

461 Court St
Carroll Gardens ⑥
+1 347 227 8227
blackgold
brooklyn.com

The incredible hotchpotch of all things weird in Black Gold Records is quintessential Brooklyn. Fuel up with their great coffee as you dig through a substantial record collection and peruse the antiques and some dusty taxidermy too. It might all seem intimidatingly cool to newcomers, but thanks to the amazing staff it immediately feels like home when you set foot in this shop. They even ship their Original Black Gold Blend worldwide.

131 **EARWAX RECORDS**

167 N 9th St
Williamsburg ①
+1 718 486 3771
earwaxrecords.net

Earwax Records opened in 1990 and is the oldest record store in Brooklyn, specializing in new and used vinyl. They have a very eclectic selection of new vinyl, with lesser known and obscure stuff, as well as a collection of vintage hi-fi equipment, including turntables, receivers, speakers, etc., all reasonably priced.

132 **BROOKLYN RECORD EXCHANGE**

599 Johnson
Avenue
East Williams-
burg ②
+1 646 969 2030
brooklynrecord
exchange.com

This store is not about a particular niche, a particular scene or a particular genre. Brooklyn Record Exchange aims to be as inclusive as possible by welcoming people who are looking for a record to play with dinner as well as serious collectors and DJs. They also offer obscure movies and books of all genres. The space with its sleek wooden interior and lots of natural light is the perfect environment for a long day of digging.

134 AFRICAN RECORD STORE

133 CAPTURED TRACKS SHOP

195 Calyer St
Greenpoint ①
+1 718 609 0871
capturedtracks.com

This is the retail record shop from Brooklyn label *Captured Tracks*. They buy, trade and sell new and used vinyl, CDs, zines and cassettes, plus monthly curated artists booths. It is a record store for people who truly are passionate about music and everything that goes with it. The people who hang out here are musicians, artists and DJs, even the staff are total musos.

134 AFRICAN RECORD CENTRE

1194 Nostrand
Avenue
Prospect Lefferts
Gardens ⑦
+1 718 493 4500

The Francis brothers' African Record Centre was founded in 1969 as a North American distributor of African music. No new releases here, only a who's who of great African music of the 1960s, 70s, 80s and maybe 90s. All records are originals, no bootlegs here. If you are looking for rare African grooves, the owners will let you listen to a record before making a purchase. LPs are 25 dollar, which sounds a bit steep but everything here is in perfect condition, with some very rare finds on offer.

135 THE MIXTAPE SHOP

1129 Bedford
Avenue
Bedford-
Stuyvesant ⑤
+1 347 529 0222
themixtapeshop.com

Classic record stores tend to be shabby, requiring you to browse through a clutter of titles in various bins. They are usually frequented by avid music fans who know what they are looking for. This cafe-cum-record store wants to be more welcoming to people. They have a clean, minimal and airy cafe with white painted hardwood floors and lots of light. Beyond the bar is an open space where you can discover the latest dance, jazz and hip-hop vinyl at reasonable prices.

CONSIGNMENT BROOKLYN

FASHION

Creative **VINTAGE CLOTHING** *stores*

136 **AMARCORD VINTAGE FASHION**

223 Bedford Avenue
Williamsburg ⓘ
+1 718 963 4001
amarcordvintage fashion.com

A beautiful collection of upscale European vintage clothing and accessories from the 1940s to the 1980s, with famous labels as well as undiscovered manufacturers. That is what makes Amarcord so cool. It's not just 'old stuff' that you'll find here but vintage that tells a story. The carefully curated and vetted merchandise is brought back from buying trips to Europe – mainly Italy, the homeland of the owners.

137 **ANTOINETTE**

119 Grand St
Williamsburg ⓘ
+1 718 387 8664
www.antoinette brooklyn.com

Antoinette mainly sells vintage items, as well as pieces by independent local designers. Lexi, the owner, is adored by everyone and will help shoppers find the best outfit for any occasion. She named the shop after her mother who worked in fashion in New York City for many years. Every piece of vintage clothing came from her mom's personal collection. Prices are affordable except for rare or designer pieces. Check the one-dollar bin for great deals, or score a quality pair of 70s jeans in the denim section.

138 BEACON'S CLOSET

92 5th Avenue
Park Slope ⑥
+1 718 230 1630
beaconscloset.com

Beacon's Closet, a female founded company that embraces sustainability and ethical business practices, buys, sells and trades vintage and contemporary clothing. This means that the inventory at Beacon's is entirely built off what customers sell to buyers at the store. It's kind of a goldmine, with current top designers or simply unique pieces. The store is known for its great deals, so expect a line outside on the weekends if you're buying or selling. There are four locations: Greenpoint, Park Slope, Bushwick and Manhattan.

139 CHICKEE'S VINTAGE

135 Wythe Avenue
Williamsburg ①
+1 239 595 8845
chickeesvintage.com

The back room of this innovative shop, run by former model and vintage aficionado Kathleen Sorbara, feels more like a living room where you hang out with your friend while shopping for your new favorite vintage finds. The small selection of vintage clothing is fun, with cheeky sweaters, pieces featuring comic book figures (Mickey Mouse, Betty Boop), vintage 501s, vintage art museum tees, Gucci loafers, and 1980s/1990s designer slacks. A real passion of love!

140 CONSIGNMENT BROOKLYN

371 Atlantic
Avenue
Boerum Hill ④
+1 718 522 3522
*consignment
brooklyn.com*

Consignment is not your typical thrift shop. The owner Eva Gentry has an extraordinary eye, and you can trust that everything on the floor was hand-picked for quality. The store offers designer and alt-designer clothes, shoes and bags for a fraction of what you would pay in retail. On any given day, you will find Marni, Stella McCartney, Ann Demeulemeester, Dries Van Noten, Helmut Lang and Alexander Wang. The clothes are impeccable, and often have never been worn.

141 FANTASY EXPLOSION

AT: THE MINI MALL
218 Bedford
Avenue
Williamsburg ①
fantasyexplosion.com

Chances are that Fantasy Explosion no longer has their pop-up at the above address, but they truly are one of the most exceptional vintage stores in Brooklyn. Check out their website and Instagram *(@fantasyexplosion)* when new vintage drops on Fridays. You will find NYC ephemera like cheesy NYC tourist T-shirts from the 80s or rare gear that is only given out to MTA workers. Check it out if you're a New Yorker who wants to show off a sense of pride with something different from the standard Yankee outfit, or if you're a tourist looking for a unique New York souvenir to take home.

142 FRONT GENERAL STORE

143 Front St
Dumbo ③
+1 646 573 0123
frontgeneralstore.com

This well curated Dumbo antique/vintage store sells old American vintage clothes as well as stationery, accessories and home decor. Japanese owner Hideya Sagawa has an incredible eye for military, workwear, denim and high-end vintage fashion, and likes to mix Japanese points of view with an old American look and feel. Make sure to take a couple of hours to get lost, touch and feel the items, and try them on in this hipper than hip boutique.

143 RUGGED ROAD & CO.

218 Bedford
Avenue
Williamsburg ①
ruggedroad-bklyn.com

It's a small store but a good place to strike gold. They stock very authentic vintage Americana clothing like military jackets, flannel shirts, vintage aloha shirts and T-shirts, college ephemera, but also eyewear, home goods and records – all around cool stuff. Everything will have some history and be in great condition, at very reasonable prices.

144 L TRAIN VINTAGE (URBAN JUNGLE)

120 Knickerbocker
Avenue
East Williams-
burg ②
+1 718 366 2200
ltrainvintagenyc.com

There are seven L Train Vintage stores in Brooklyn, and they are all a thrifter's paradise. This is the perfect place for anyone searching for cool vintage clothing on a budget. Don't expect to find big-name brands like rare Tommy Hilfiger, Lacoste or Abercrombie, but an entire nineties outfit for less than 100 dollar should be doable. When visiting an L Train store, never stop digging and take your time because those much-coveted gems are hard to find immediately.

142 FRONT GENERAL STORE

Lovely **BOUTIQUES**
for clothes and more

---

145 **A. CHENG**

466 Bergen St
Park Slope ⑥
+1 718 783 2826
achengshop.com

A. Cheng is a cute boutique that's hip without being obnoxious. Dressy, work-appropriate womenswear designed by Alice Cheng that is affordable, well-made, and polished without looking like it comes from the Upper East Side; a perfectly imperfect look. Besides carrying the A. Cheng house label, the boutique also sells 30 other labels and jewelry by local designers, all carefully selected and sharing Cheng's cheekily altered uptown sensibility.

146 **BEDSTUYFLY**

287 Ralph Avenue
Bedford-
Stuyvesant ⑤
+1 347 406 9927
bedstuyfly.com

This super hip, laidback boutique offers an independent line of Brooklyn-themed urban streetwear with cool graphic tees, hats, jackets and sweat pants for men and women. Owner Stephen Usenbor, who goes by the name 'S. King', opened the store in 2009 and expanded it in 2013 by purchasing the townhouse next door. There's another location further down the road at 1407 Fulton Street.

147 BHOOMKI

158 5th Avenue
Park Slope ⑥
+1 718 857 5245
bhoomki.com

Walk into this little oasis and find the most elegant clothing dedicated to environmental and/or social responsibility, including the designs by its gorgeous owner, Swati Argade. Pretty silk dresses, sweaters, easy jumpsuits, and bold jewelry, at prices that are in the reasonable range. Bhoomki partners with companies that support traditional artisanship in over 18 countries, and Argade's own collection is known for incorporating sustainable fabrics with classic and tailored silhouettes. Pieces are manufactured mainly in New York's Garment District or by fairly paid artisans in other countries.

148 M.PATMOS

380 Atlantic
Avenue
Boerum Hill ④
+1 718 855 1303
mpatmos.com

Housed in a beautiful brownstone with tin ceilings and wood floors, M.PATOS, or Marcia Patos, is known for modern yet timeless knits and styles. Her own designs are luxurious and lavish, and she mixes them in her store with other independent brands, as well as with interesting jewelry, accessories, coffee table books, and home and gift items. M.PATMOS clothing is sold at high-end boutiques in the USA, Japan and Canada, but it all comes from Brooklyn.

149 SINCERELY, TOMMY

343 Tompkins
Avenue
Bedford-
Stuyvesant ⑤
+1 718 484 8484
sincerelytommy.com

In 2014, at the age of 26, Kai Avent-deLeon opened Sincerely, Tommy in her community of Bed-Stuy. This cult-favorite fashion and lifestyle boutique carries a lovely selection of emerging womenswear – often from local designers or discovered on travels around the world –, artful jewelry and stylish pieces for the home, all with a focus on community. The sunny cafe and workspace offer excellent coffee too.

150 SOULA SHOES

185 Smith St
Boerum Hill ④
+1 718 834 8423
soulashoes.com

Owner Rick Lee learned the tricks at places like Lord & Taylor, Charles Jourdan and Charivari, but most of all as a buyer at Barneys New York. He spent months in shoe factories and show rooms all over Europe looking for the best shoes. All of this until he decided to set up his own shop in his beloved neighborhood of Boerum Hill in 2004. Over the years, this small boutique became an institution and destination for countless travel and fashion bloggers. The place to go for the best selection of shoes for men and women.

151 THANK YOU HAVE A GOOD DAY

392 Van Brunt St
Red Hook ⑥
+1 718 669 6854
*thankyouhave
agoodday.com*

Thank You Have A Good Day is a boutique that sells primarily items that can only be found at Thank You Have a Good Day, or as they say 'an intimate space filled with considered and cohesive collections of objects we don't want to live without'. This includes their own handmade and one-of-a-kind clothing collection, vintage work jackets and sweaters, but also some ceramics, jewelry, vinegar, home goods, and apothecary items. Their studio is just one block away, so there's a constant influx of new things.

One-of-a-kind **HOME DECORATION** *stores*

152 **BEAM**

272 Kent Avenue
Williamsburg ①
+1 646 450 1469
beambk.com

Art and design lovers, Ali Arain and Greg Coccaro, travel the world to discover the best of the best in furniture, lighting, art, home goods, and gifts. They are also committed to finding and showcasing local designers. A returning theme in their store is color, a sense of humor, a mix of high and low, and New York smart. But quality, craftsmanship and good design always come first. This is the perfect shop to stumble upon what you really need, or to find a few things you'd never expect.

153 **COLLYER'S MANSION**

179 Atlantic
Avenue
Brooklyn Heights ④
+1 347 987 3342
shopthemansion.com

Named after the Collyer brothers, two American brothers who became infamous for their compulsive hoarding, this perfect home goods store carries a curated and eclectic collection of artisan-made goods from makers both local and farther abreast, including midcentury-style and eco-friendly furniture, ceramics, lighting, vibrant textiles, original artwork, handmade jewelry and more. The art on the walls is re-hung often, and the stock changes frequently too.

154 FENG SWAY

41 Norman Avenue
Greenpoint ①
+1 917 480 0636
fengsway.com

Completely run by a self-proclaimed 'girl gang' of artists and designers, this bohemian dreamland in the middle of Greenpoint sells gorgeous exotic plants and planters, antique furniture, excellent and rare vintage clothing, and other fun bits and pieces in a giant industrial space. They also have a very extensive online collection.

155 GREENERY UNLIMITED

91 West St
Greenpoint ①
+1 646 543 3797
greenery unlimited.co

The only goal that owners Rebecca Bullene and Adam Besheer of Greenery Unlimited had was to bring the outdoors in. This unique tropical paradise showcases green installations and botanic design concepts, but most of all, they give New Yorkers the tools and knowledge to keep plants alive. Fully integrating plants as part of the living space, and thus increase the quality of life, is what they call 'biophilic design'. They have a thriving online presence and an impressive client list that ranges from the likes of TED Talks and Google to The New York Times and Netflix...

156 PEACE + RIOT

401-403 Tompkins
Avenue
Bedford-
Stuyvesant ⑤
+1 347 663 6100
peaceandriot.com

This eclectic and global design store – run by Bed-Stuy native and interior decorator Achuziam Maha-Sanchez and her husband, Lionel Sanchez – stocks beautifully crafted African and Caribbean home goods, exquisite jewelry, funky wood coasters, Brooklyn-themed umbrella holders, Brooklyn tote bags and colorful items from North and West Africa. All in all, a bit of everything but everything thoughtfully chosen.

157 THE PRIMARY ESSENTIALS

372 Atlantic
Avenue
Boerum Hill ④
+1 718 522 1804
*theprimary
essentials.com*

Former stylist-turned-business owner Lauren Snyder is the mastermind behind this beautiful artisanal home goods and gift store on Brooklyn's Atlantic Avenue. The ultimate gift shop, it sells a curated collection of well-designed, artisanal-yet-functional takes on the essential items that we use in our daily lives. Ceramics, jewelry, textiles, beauty products, books, and other unique finds are made by independent, craft-based designers and artisans – both locally and abroad. Lauren is so close with many of her designers that they consult her directly on their limited-run goods, just for her shop.

Where to find that
VINTAGE FURNITURE

158 CITYFOUNDRY

369 Atlantic
Avenue
Boerum Hill ④
+1 718 923 1786
cityfoundry.com

cityFoundry opened in 2000 and set the tone for
the now established design scene in this area of
Brooklyn. The collection consists of midcentury
modern and industrial-influenced furniture,
lighting, and objets d'art. Custom upholstery and
furniture restoration are also available. In addition
to the multiple storefront shop on Atlantic Avenue,
there is a showroom and warehouse location
in Prospect Heights, which can be visited by
appointment only.

159 HOME UNION

319 Graham
Avenue
Williamsburg ①
+1 347 987 4899
homeunionnyc.com

When Meghan Lavery and Daniel King, the owners
of Home Union, get their hands on a rare piece
of vintage furniture they simultaneously list it
on their website and announce the news to their
200.000 Instagram followers, and the piece sells
in seconds. This cult-favorite vintage store was
founded in 2016 as a way to share the vintage finds
Meghan and Daniel had been collecting. They have
a passion for 20th-century design and one-of-a-
kind treasures. You will also find a lovely array of
contemporary candles, soaps, and framed prints.

160 COPPER+PLAID

655 Manhattan
Avenue
Greenpoint ①
+1 717 379 5666

This well-curated small boutique with midcentury and Danish modern furniture is a great place to start your search for comfortable and beautiful pieces. New furniture arrives almost daily and the pieces are in near-perfect-to-perfect condition. Erica, the owner, hand-picks all the furniture with the strongest aesthetic and originality. Open during the weekend and by appointment during the week only. They deliver in NYC.

161 OPEN AIR MODERN

489 Lorimer St
Williamsburg ①
+1 718 383 6465
openairmodern.com

According to Matt Singer, the owner, you must surround yourself with objects you love. These objects can be found at Open Air Modern in the revamped garage in Williamsburg. About 2000 books on design and art are stacked on architectural-framed shelves and midcentury modern furniture has taken over the large warehouse space. Matt also advices on how to restore furniture and helps choose appropriate fabric for any upholstery job.

162 OTHER TIMES VINTAGE

48 Bogart St
East Williams-
burg ②
+1 917 922 1159
othertimes
vintage.com

Other Times Vintage showcases its midcentury modern furnishings and decor in a spacious loft space with gorgeous, vaulted ceilings. On offer are a curated selection of furniture, plants – sanseveria, cacti, triostar stromanthe, fiddle-leaf figs and palms –, ceramics and rugs. They clean up, repair, and refinish all their vintage items before they start a new life in a new home. There's also a cool selection of vintage books.

163 VAN DER MOST MODERN

159 Troutman St
Bushwick ②
+1 323 640 2109
*vandermost
modern.com*

This midcentury furniture shop in Bushwick offers an eclectic collection of furniture and decor pieces carefully curated by Dutch founder and owner Gijs van der Most. As a photographer who grew up in the Netherlands, Gijs developed a strong sense of aesthetics and taste, allowing him to curate the incredible collection of quality materials with a clean, simple aesthetic that are featured in his shop.

ONE SOUTH FIRST (1S1)

BUILDINGS 🏢

The **BRIDGES** of Brooklyn

164 **BROOKLYN BRIDGE**
Brooklyn Heights ④

The Brooklyn Bridge, with its recognizable Gothic arches and limestone, granite towers must be one of the most brilliant structures in New York City and is an engineering marvel. It spans the East River, connecting Manhattan and Brooklyn, and is 1.8 kilometers long. The bridge opened in 1883 and was, at that time, the longest suspension bridge in the world. You can cross it by car or bicycle, but the most rewarding option is walking. Go at sunset from Brooklyn to Manhattan, and experience the most stunning views of New York. Climb the stairs at the underpass on Cadman Plaza East (between Sands Street and Prospect Street) in Dumbo to reach the pedestrian lane. The long-awaited separate bike lane opened only in September 2021.

165 MANHATTAN BRIDGE

Dumbo ③

The last of the three suspension bridges built across the lower East River is the Manhattan Bridge. It opened in 1909 and connects Chinatown in Manhattan with Downtown Brooklyn. Pedestrians, cyclists and automobiles can cross the steel structure, but it is also one of the few bridges to carry trains. Situated between the Brooklyn Bridge and the Williamsburg Bridge, a walk across the Manhattan Bridge gives an excellent view of all three bridges. Immortalized on Sergio Leone's *Once Upon a Time in America*'s movie poster, the bridge seen from the intersection of Water Street and Washington Street in Dumbo, has become one of the most instagrammable spots in NYC. The pedestrian entrance is on the corner of Sands Street and Jay Street in Downtown Brooklyn.

166 PULASKI BRIDGE

Greenpoint

If you are a runner, it is a good to know that once you have crossed the Pulaski Bridge you have passed the halfway point of the New York City Marathon. This red bascule bridge connects Greenpoint in Brooklyn to Long Island City in Queens over Newtown Creek. The name of the bridge, which opened in 1954, refers to Polish military commander and American Revolutionary War fighter Casimir Pułaski and honors the large Polish-American population of Greenpoint. Walk or cycle over the bridge to enjoy views of the industrial areas surrounding Newtown Creek as well as the beautiful skyline of Manhattan.

167 VERRAZZANO-NARROWS BRIDGE

Bay Ridge ⑧

The Verrazzano-Narrows Bridge, NYC's tallest bridge, spans The Narrows from Brooklyn to Staten Island. It took five years to build and opened in 1964. Unfortunately, this magnificent bridge is only open to bikers, walkers, and cyclists on special occasions like the New York City Marathon. But, because of the bridge's tremendous height (211 meters), you can see it from almost any point near Brooklyn's southern end. The best views of the bridge (with sunset) can be had from the promenade in Bay Ridge's Shore Road Park. Fun fact: it was only in 2018 that Governor Cuomo signed legislation adding a second letter 'z' to the bridge's name, which had been misspelled for over 50 years.

168 WILLIAMSBURG BRIDGE

Williamsburg ①

The Williamsburg Bridge, a suspension bridge that connects the Lower East Side of Manhattan to Brooklyn's South Williamsburg, opened in 1903 to pedestrians, bicycles, and horse-drawn carriages. It was the second bridge, after the Brooklyn Bridge, to be built over the East River. The chief engineer Leffert Buck, was said to be inspired by the Eiffel Tower in his design of the bridge, which is apparent in its towers. These days you can walk, cycle, drive or take the subway. Pedestrians, who should enter at Berry Street between South 5th Street and South 6th Street have their own walkway but need to stick to their lane.

The **OLDEST HOUSES**

in Brooklyn

169 **HENDRICK I. LOTT HOUSE** (1720)

1940 E 36th St
Marine Park ⑧
lotthouse.org

In the not-so-hip area of Marine Park, a neighborhood of police officers, firefighters, postal workers and city employees, you can still visit the Hendrick I. Lott House, one of fourteen remaining Dutch Colonial farmhouses in Brooklyn. The Lott family emigrated from Holland and acquired the land in 1652. The oldest portion of the house, built by Johannes Lott in 1720, was incorporated in the current building that was constructed in 1800 by Johannes' grandson Hendrick. The Lotts relied on the labor of slaves, but freed their slaves by 1805, years before the abolition of slavery in New York State in 1827. Later, the house may have served as a stop on the Underground Railroad. The last Lott family member lived here until her death in 1989. The Lott House is currently closed for renovation but tours can be arranged by emailing *FLH@lotthouse.org*. The yard and house can be viewed from outside the fence.

170 THE LEFFERTS HOMESTEAD (1783)

452 Flatbush
Avenue
Prospect Park ⑦
+1 718 789 2822
prospectpark.org

In 1660, Dutch immigrant Pieterse van Hagewout founded a farm in the rural area at the northern edge of the town of Flatbush. But the actual Lefferts Homestead was built by Lefferts' descendent Peter Lefferts around 1783. It was built on the corner of Maple Street and Flatbush Avenue in what is now called Prospect Lefferts Gardens, and stayed in the Lefferts family until 1918. It was then donated to the City of New York which moved it to Prospect Park. The Prospect Park Alliance operates and preserves this important piece of NYC's heritage. Unfortunately, you can only see the outside of this historic house as it is currently closed for restoration.

171 THE PIETER CLAESEN WYCKOFF HOUSE (1652)

5816 Clarendon
Road
East Flatbush ⑧
+1 718 629 5400
wyckoffmuseum.org

In East Flatbush, an area of Brooklyn mostly populated by working-class Brooklynites, stands the Pieter Claesen Wyckoff House. It is the oldest surviving Dutch saltbox house in America. A saltbox is a wooden frame house with a long, pitched roof that slopes down to the back. The building was altered and restored over time, but the original one-room structure from before 1641, where Pieter Claesen Wyckoff and his wife Grietje van Ness raised 11 children, can still be visited. Descendants of the Wyckoff family donated it to the city of New York in the 1980s. Now, the house is completely restored and open to the public. It has three beautiful period rooms that illustrate how the Wyckoff family lived in the early 19th century.

172 THE WYCKOFF-BENNETT-MONT HOMESTEAD
(1766)
1669 E 22nd St
Madison ⑧

The Wyckoff-Bennett Homestead, a farmhouse
built before the Revolutionary War, is located in
the sleepy residential area of Madison, a neighborhood with a large population of Chinese and Soviet
residents. The white-shingle, city landmarked
house that Hendrick and Abraham Wyckoff built
around 1766, has a porch with a distinctive Dutch
Colonial-style curved roof. The homestead housed
Hessian soldiers – German soldiers who served
as auxiliaries to the British Army – during the
American Revolution. It is one of the last privately
owned Dutch Colonial houses in New York City.
If you know the owners, you can perhaps visit it.

CLASSIC *constructions*

173 BROOKLYN HISTORICAL SOCIETY

128 Pierrepont St
Brooklyn Heights ④
+1 718 222 4111
brooklynhistory.org

The magnificent Queen Anne-style landmark building that houses the Brooklyn Historical Society dates from 1881 and was designed by one of NYC's finest architects, George Browne Post. Unlike Post's more familiar classical buildings, like the NY Stock Exchange Building, this marvel with its bright terracotta façade and intricate brickwork, is adorned with terracotta busts of famous people including Shakespeare and Beethoven, all made by American sculptor Olin Levy Warner. The landmarked library interior carries an impressive collection of materials, and features elaborately carved woodwork, original furnishings and stained-glass windows. The exhibition space and library are open to the public.

174 BROOKLYN PUBLIC LIBRARY

10 Grand Army Plaza
Prospect Heights ⑤
+1 718 230 2100
bklynlibrary.org/
locations/central

Considered one of America's greatest art deco buildings, even though ground broke for the original Brooklyn library in 1912, it didn't open to the public until 1941, owing to the Great Depression following World War I. The library's design evokes an open book, with its spine on Grand Army Plaza and two wings opening like pages onto Eastern Parkway and Flatbush Avenue. The seemingly sky-high wooden front doors are adorned with fifteen gilt figures from American literature, framed by columns with gold-leaf etchings. They depict the evolution of art and science through the age, a majestic paean to literature and education.

175 EAGLE WAREHOUSE & STORAGE COMPANY

28 Old Fulton St
Dumbo ③

The Eagle Warehouse in Dumbo is slightly reminiscent of the Palazzo Vecchio in Florence. This medieval brick fortress, completed in 1894, was designed by Brooklyn star architect Frank Freeman. He created a number of buildings in neighboring Brooklyn Heights, including the wonderful Herman Behr Mansion on Pierrepont Street, as well as the demolished Hotel Margaret. This landmarked warehouse has a massive entry arch, barred windows and machicolated moldings, and was used for a variety of purposes. Eventually it was converted into luxury apartments in 1980.

176 LITCHFIELD VILLA

95 Prospect
Park West
Prospect Park ⑦
+1 718 965 8951
nycgo.com/venues/
prospect-park-
litchfield-villa

This 19th-century mansion, a hidden gem in Prospect Park, was once an elegant family home. It was designed long before the park was created by one of New York's architectural greats, the Gothic Revivalist Alexander Jackson Davis, and commissioned by Edwin C. and Grace Litchfield. The land and house were taken against the family's wishes in 1868 for the creation of Prospect Park. The Litchfield family were given permission to stay on as tenants and, according to park records, paid 2500 dollar per year in rent in 1883. The building now houses the administrative offices for the Prospect Park Alliance.

177 PARACHUTE JUMP

Riegelmann
Boardwalk
Coney Island ⑧

The Coney Island Parachute Jump – also called Brooklyn's Eiffel Tower – was originally built for the 1939 New York World's Fair in Queens, and was moved to Steeplechase Park in Coney Island in 1941. The 76-meter-tall steel framed structure was an amusement ride where riders were strapped into a two-person seat, lifted to the top, and dropped. The parachute and shock absorbers at the bottom would slow their descent. The Parachute Jump ride ceased to operate in 1964 when the Steeplechase park closed permanently. It has since remained a permanent landmark on the Coney Island skyline.

178 THE BOATHOUSE

101 East Drive
Prospect Park ⑦
+1 646 393 9031
prospectpark.org

The Beaux Arts landmark with its graceful arches and Guastavino ceiling tiles was built in 1905 and overlooks the scenic Lullwater in Prospect Park. During the 20th century the Boathouse was used for a number of purposes but was not maintained. By 1964, after years of deterioration, the building was almost demolished, but a group of Brooklyn preservationists, including Brooklyn poet Marianne Moore, managed to save it (just 48 hours before it was scheduled to be torn down!). The renovated Boathouse now houses the Audubon Center and is one of Prospect Park's most popular buildings.

179 THE PRISON SHIP MARTYRS' MONUMENT

AT: FORT GREENE PARK
Willoughby
Avenue and
Washington Park
Fort Greene ④
+1 718 965 8900
*nycgovparks.org/
parks*

This 45-meter-tall monument to the Prison Ship Martyrs of the American Revolution, by Stanford White, consists of a 30-meter-wide granite staircase and a central Doric column. It honors the more than 11.500 men and women who died as captives of war during America's fight for independence. They were jailed on 16 British prison ships moored along Brooklyn's shores in Wallabout Bay – now Brooklyn Navy Yard – and died in horrendous conditions. Their bodies were tossed overboard or hastily buried along the shore. Ultimately, the remains of the prisoners were moved to Fort Greene Park in 1873 and in 1908, President-elect William Howard Taft attended the monument's dedication.

Remarkable **HOUSES** *of* **WORSHIP**

180 **BASILICA OF OUR LADY OF PERPETUAL HELP**

526 59th St
Sunset Park ⑦
+1 718 492 9200
olphbkny.org

The parish of Our Lady of Perpetual Help was established by Bishop Charles Edward McDonnell in 1892. The construction of the current Romanesque, granite church with a limestone exterior by architect Franz Joseph Untersee, began in 1907. It was designated a minor Basilica in 1969. At the time of its completion the parish was largely Irish in character, but today it is predominantly Hispanic and Chinese.

181 **EMMANUEL BAPTIST CHURCH**

279 Lafayette Avenue
Clinton Hill ⑤
+1 718 622 1107
ebcconnects.com

The French Gothic designed Emmanuel Baptist Church, a megachurch in Clinton Hill founded in 1881, has one of New York's most spectacular church interiors. With its rich mixture of stained glass, wood and elaborate stencil work it is one of Brooklyn's finest architectural treasures. The architect is Francis Kimball, who is a major name in late 19th-century NYC architecture. In 1981, the Landmarks Preservation Commission designated the church as part of the Clinton Hill Historic District.

182 FLATBUSH REFORMED DUTCH CHURCH

890 Flatbush Avenue
Flatbush ⑦
+1 718 284 5140

One of the oldest churches in Brooklyn is the Flatbush Reformed Dutch Church that was originally built in the shape of a cross in 1654 by order of Peter Stuyvesant. The second church was erected on the same site in 1698, and the third, a 2,5-story stone Federal-style building was designed by Thomas Fardon in 1798. The tower's clock and bell date back to 1796 and were made in the Netherlands. The bell has tolled for the death of every United States President and Vice President. Each Sunday morning at 10.30 am the community of Christians come together for a service.

183 NEW UTRECHT REFORMED CHURCH

1827 84th St
Bensonhurst ⑧
+1 718 236 0678
newutrechtchurch.org

The first New Utrecht Reformed Church building was constructed in 1700. It formerly stood at a different location. The present church, using the stones from the original church, was built in the Gothic Revival style in 1828. It was one of the first buildings to be designated a National Historic Landmark in 1966. The Liberty Pole, the sixth on the site of the present church, was originally erected in 1783 at the end of the Revolutionary War to harass departing British troops.

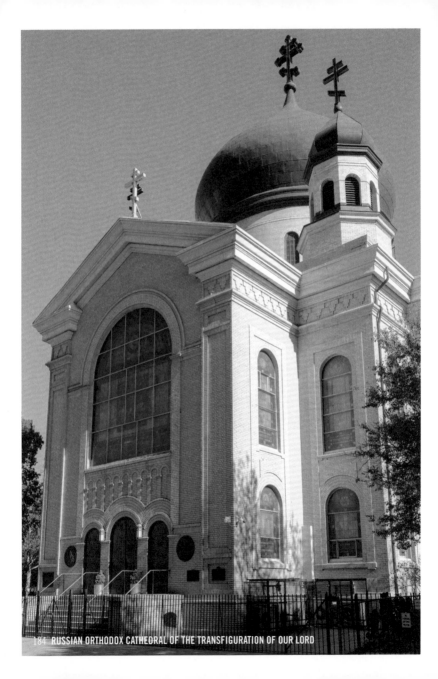

184 RUSSIAN ORTHODOX CATHEDRAL OF THE TRANSFIGURATION OF OUR LORD

228 N 12th St
Williamsburg ⓘ
+1 718 387 1064
roct.org

The Russian Orthodox Cathedral of the Transfiguration of Our Lord is one of the largest churches in the New York Metropolitan area and a NYC Landmark. It was designed by Louis Allmendiger and opened in 1922. The 5 copper cupolas topped with Patriarchal crosses are visible far and wide. It is the only example of its kind of Byzantine Revival architecture in NYC. The founders of this parish came from Galicia, which is located in the southeastern section of today's Poland. Fun fact, exterior shots of the cathedral were once used in an episode of the popular tv-series *Seinfeld*.

185 THE PARK CHURCH CO-OP

129 Russell St
Green Point ⓘ
+1 917 426 1596
parkchurchcoop.org

The Park Church Co-op is a Lutheran ministry founded in 2015 and located in an historic church building (erected in 1908), the former Lutheran Church of the Messiah. The Park Church Co-op aims to create a culture of radical openness toward all, and its building provides a space for local music and art, a shelter for people in need, and a spiritual sanctuary for the entire community. Membership is open to anyone of any religious persuasion, including all atheists.

186 ST. ANN & THE HOLY TRINITY CHURCH

157 Montague St
Brooklyn Heights ④
+1 718 875 6960
stannholytrinity.org

Construction of The Church of the Holy Trinity began in 1844 on the highest point in Brooklyn Heights. This important example of Gothic Revival architecture is notable for its elaborately vaulted roof and extensive suite of stained-glass windows by William Jay Bolton. A disagreement within the congregation during the Cold War led to the dissolution of the church, and the building was closed and stood mostly vacant for more than a decade. In 1969, nearby St. Ann's Church was permitted to move four blocks into the long-empty Holy Trinity building and therefore is now known as St. Ann & the Holy Trinity Church.

187 ST. BARBARA'S ROMAN CATHOLIC CHURCH

138 Bleecker St
Bushwick ②
+1 718 452 3660
stbarbara-brooklyn.org

Designed in 1907 by architects Helmle and Huberty, St. Barbara's Roman Catholic Church is an early example of Spanish baroque or plateresque style. Constructed of yellow brick and gleaming white terracotta, the church soars above the low-rise residences of the surrounding area, and is the most prominent structure in Bushwick. The plateresque style was brought to the New World by early Spanish settlers in Mexico and the American Southwest. St. Barbara's is modeled after the mission churches built in these regions. Founded in 1893 as a German Parish, St. Barbara's has served successive generations of immigrants.

SKYSCRAPERS *and* MODERN *buildings*

188 325 KENT

325 Kent Avenue
Williamsburg ①
+1 646 535 8992
325kent.com

325 Kent, which was built in 2017, is one of South Williamsburg's newest premier waterfront addresses and the first residential building the architectural firm, SHoP, has completed as part of their Domino Park master plan. Occupants enjoy expansive views of New York City's breathtaking skyline from pricey apartments facing the river, as well as from the rooftop. But the best view from the entire building is from John V. Lindsay East River Park in Manhattan.

189 COURT CHAMBERS BUILDING

75 Livingston St
Brooklyn Heights ④

The 30-story, landmarked art deco building – also called the Brooklyn Chamber of Commerce Building or the wedding cake building – is one of Brooklyn's first skyscrapers and was designed by Ukraine-born architect Abraham J. Simberg. This neo-Gothic office tower, built in 1926, was converted into cooperative apartments in 1981. The top-floor apartments are extremely costly but do come with the most stunning views of New York Harbor, the Verrazzano-Narrows Bridge, Lower Manhattan, the Statue of Liberty and Ellis Island.

190 BROOKLYN POINT

1 City Point
Downtown
Brooklyn ④
+1 718 962 0267
*brooklynpoint
nyc.com*

With its 68 floors and 219-meter tower, the Brooklyn Point, designed by Kohn Pedersen Fox architects, is the tallest building in Brooklyn (at the time of writing in 2020). The tower contains 458 residences with a selection of studio to three-bedroom luxury apartments. At the top of the tower is the city's highest rooftop infinity pool, offering sweeping views of the Brooklyn and Manhattan skylines.

191 ONE SOUTH FIRST (1S1)

1 S 1st St
Williamsburg ①
+1 718 736 2871
onesouthfirst.com

The interlocking iconic towers of One South First (1S1), built in 2019, are located at the northern end of the newly developed Domino Park at the Williamsburg waterfront. The dramatic and handsome 45-story mixed-use tower, designed by COOKFOX Architects, comprises 332 luxury waterfront rentals, retail and work spaces, all with exceptional views, details, and tons of amenities.

192 WILLIAMSBURGH SAVINGS BANK TOWER

1 Hanson Place
Fort Greene ④

This historic skyscraper was built in 1927 by the architectural firm Halsey, McCormack and Helmer as the new headquarters for the Williamsburgh Savings Bank. The slender tower, with its detailed Romanesque-Byzantine arches, columns and capitals, features a gilded copper dome and a magnificent lobby. Up until 2010 this was the tallest building in Brooklyn, and the four-faced clock at the top of the building, remains one of the world's largest. The bank tower was converted into upmarket residences in the late 2000s. Unfortunately, the building's observation deck with its magnificent views is no longer open to the public.

DITMAS PARK

DISCOVER 👣

Discover **H I S T O R I C**
Brooklyn Heights

193 **58 JORALEMON STREET**

58 Joralemon St
Brooklyn Heights ④

This ordinary building looks just like the neighboring townhouses. However, behind its blacked-out windows, no one is at home and nobody has been for more than 100 years. Despite its immaculate brickwork, number 58 is not a home at all. It is a ventilation point and secret exit for the NYC Subway disguised as a brownstone. Nobody really knows what was the price tag when the MTA acquired the house in 1908, but its value would be close to four million dollar according to a 2021 estimate.

194 **BROOKLYN HEIGHTS PROMENADE**

Between Orange St
and Remsen St
Brooklyn Heights ④
+1 212 639 9675
nycgovparks.org

Strolling over the Brooklyn Heights Promenade while the sun sets behind the buildings of Lower Manhattan is a unique experience and gives you the best view of Lower Manhattan, Governor's Island, the Statue of Liberty, Brooklyn Bridge Park, and other landmarks. Or just sit on a bench and wait until dark to see the whole of Manhattan lit up. This 557-meter-long esplanade built in the 1950s is still one of the most popular destinations in Brooklyn for tourists and locals alike. Take the subway to High Street (A, C) or Clark Street (2, 3), from there it's just a 7-minute walk.

195 HERMAN BEHR MANSION

82 Pierrepont St
Brooklyn Heights ④

From single-family home to boarding house, brothel, a residence for the Franciscan Brothers and currently rental apartments, the Herman Behr Mansion has seen it all. The mansion was built in 1888 for industrialist Herman Behr (whose son Karl, a renowned tennis pro, survived the sinking of the Titanic in 1912) and was designed by prominent Brooklyn architect Frank Freeman in his signature Romanesque Revival style. The exterior has a massive brownstone base and terracotta on the upper stories. Don't miss the crazy animal ornaments on the façade.

196 LOVE LANE

Between Hicks St and Henry St
Brooklyn Heights ④

One wonders how this little street got such a charming name. The story goes that in colonial times it was an Indian trail leading to the nearby East River. Or when the Dutch arrived, it became a popular path for romantic walks. Another story says that Love Lane, which is perpendicular to College Place (where the Brooklyn Collegiate Institute for Young Ladies was located) was a popular kissing spot. Boys would park their carriages there to say one last goodbye to their girlfriends before dropping them off for the night. These days, it's just a little side street that connects Henry Street to Hicks Street. It's up to current-day bachelors to take a loved one for a stroll and make Love Lane deserve its name again.

197 PLYMOUTH CHURCH OF THE PILGRIMS

57 Orange St
Brooklyn Heights ④
+1 718 624 4743
plymouthchurch.org

The founding minister of this 1849 New England-style brick church, Henry Ward Beecher, fought hard to end slavery. Beecher was the brother of Harriet Beecher Stowe, who was the author of the controversial antislavery novel *Uncle Tom's Cabin*. He was both celebrated and hated for his abolitionist points of view. The church played an important part in the Underground Railroad, a network of African American as well as white people who offered shelter and aid to escaped slaves from the South. Inside the church, a plaque at pew 89 marks the spot where Abraham Lincoln sat on 26 February 1860 to hear Beecher preach. The *Underground Railroad*, a historical fiction novel from 2016 by Colson Whitehead, tells the story of two slaves in the South during the 19th century, who make a bid for freedom.

198 TRUMAN CAPOTE'S HOUSE

70 Willow St
Brooklyn Heights ④

The yellow house at 70 Willow Street is no longer yellow. When *Grand Theft Auto* creator Dan Houser purchased the residence for a whopping 12,5 million dollar in 2012, the yellow paint was removed to expose the original brick. The house was built in 1839 and is one of the many beautiful old houses in this neighborhood, but its greatest claim to fame is that Truman Capote lived in the basement apartment from 1955 to 1965. He rented it from his friend Oliver Smith, a Broadway set designer and American Ballet Theatre co-director, and wrote part of *Breakfast at Tiffany's* as well as *In Cold Blood* here.

The FILM SETS of Brooklyn

199 DO THE RIGHT THING WAY

Between Lexington Avenue and Quincy St
Bedford-Stuyvesant ⑤

Do the Right Thing Way is named after Spike Lee's 1989 provocative film about race relations in late 1980s Bedford-Stuyvesant. Most of *Do the Right Thing* was shot in eight weeks on the residential block between Lexington Avenue and Quincy Street. You will find Mookie's home on 173 Stuyvesant Avenue and an empty lot on the corner of Stuyvesant Avenue, where the film crew built Sal's Famous Pizzeria. The iconic block was officially named Do the Right Thing Way in July 2015. It was the first time a work of art, rather than a person or an organization, was used as a secondary street name.

200 FRENCH CONNECTION CHASE

Elevated subway track above Stillwell Avenue, 86th St and New Utrecht Avenue
Bensonhurst ⑧

The famous chase in the 1971 thriller *The French Connection* was filmed below the elevated subway track on Stillwell Avenue between Bay 50th Street station and ended at 62nd Street station in the neighborhood of Bensonhurst in South Brooklyn. The chase between a car and the elevated train was shot in one take without proper permits from the city. Many of the (near) collisions were real and not planned. If you take the D train from 62nd Street to Bay 50 Street station, you can experience the route of the entire chase from inside the train.

201 MOONSTRUCK HOUSE

19 Cranberry St
Brooklyn Heights ④

The four-story Federal-style brownstone on the corner of Cranberry and Willow Streets is called the Moonstruck House because it was the location for the 1987 movie starring Cher and Nicolas Cage, for which Cher won an Oscar. The house was built in 1833 and was owned for nearly 50 years by Edwards Rullman, an architect who was influential in convincing the City of New York to declare Brooklyn Heights its first historic district in 1965.

202 SATURDAY NIGHT FEVER

Various locations
in Bay Ridge &
Bensonhurst

The opening scene of *Saturday Night Fever* is one of the most famous in cinema history. It starts with a shot of the Brooklyn Bridge with the Twin Towers in the background, followed by a bird's eye view of South Brooklyn, a shot of the Verrazzano-Narrows Bridge, ending in Bay Ridge, where we see John Travolta strolling down 86th Street to the tune of *Staying Alive* by the Bee Gees. Travolta walks into Lenny's Pizza, a place that has been in business since 1953 and still exists today (*lennyspizza86.com*).

203 SOPHIE'S CHOICE

101 Rugby Road
Flatbush ⑦

A picnic with Sophie, Nathan and Stingo in Prospect Park, a visit to the Central Library in Flatbush and the fantastic champagne scene on the Brooklyn Bridge all make the 1982 movie *Sophie's Choice* a true Brooklyn love song. But it's the boarding house at 101 Rugby Road in Flatbush that steals the show in this adaptation of William Styron's novel about a Jewish Holocaust survivor. The majestic 1903 Queen Anne-style Victorian house was painted pink for the movie. These days it's back to a much more sensible red, grey and white, but it's still there and a tourist attraction.

Unique Brooklyn
NEIGHBORHOODS

204 **BIGGIE SMALLS'**
    HOOD

226 St James Place
Clinton Hill ⑤

If you're a fan of The Notorious B.I.G. also known as Biggie Smalls, head out to Clinton Hill where it all started for this American rapper who was killed in 1997 at the age of 24. Biggie's childhood home was at 226 St James Place (now also called Christopher "Notorious B.I.G." Wallace Way). The neighborhood has changed considerably since, but plenty of landmarks are still there. His local barber *Respect for Life* at 932-A Fulton Street and his favorite diner Country House Diner at 887 Fulton Street. Don't miss the 38-foot (12-meter) mural by artists Naoufal Alaoui and Scott Zimmerman on the corner of Bedford Avenue and Quincy Street.

205 **CEMETERY BELT**

833 Jamaica Ave
Cypress Hills
+1 718 277 2900
*cypresshills
cemetery.org*

In 1852, when Manhattan's population began to explode and places to bury people became scarce, all burial sites on the island were prohibited. That is why the undeveloped area along the 2,5-mile (4-kilometer) Queens-Brooklyn border became the primary destination for the dead. The now more than a dozen cemeteries there, collectively called the Cemetery Belt, have many more dead residents than living ones. The actress Mae West, the baseball player Jackie Robinson, and the Dutch artist Piet Mondrian have their resting place in *Cypress Hills National Cemetery* while the magician Harry Houdini was buried (not alive, mind) in *Machpelah Cemetery* in Queens.

206 **CONEY ISLAND**

Coney Island
+1 718 372 5159
coneyisland.com

Everyone should visit Coney Island at least once. Located on a peninsula in the southernmost part of Brooklyn, it offers plenty of tacky entertainment as well as packed beaches in the summer. The most famous attractions are the Cyclone roller coaster and the Wonder Wheel at Luna Park, the legendary Nathan's Famous 4th of July hot-dog eating contest, an eccentric Mermaid Parade in June, and much more. Don't expect sophistication, but a lot of fun! In wintertime, when most attractions are closed, walking beside the Atlantic Ocean on the 4,3-kilometer boardwalk could well be one of the most scenic walks in Brooklyn.

207 DITMAS PARK
Flatbush

The Ditmas Park Historic District at the southern tip of Prospect Park was developed in 1902 by realtor Lewis H. Pounds and is one of Brooklyn's most beautiful neighborhoods. It is known for its majestic single-family houses built in the Colonial Revival style. Wonderful stand-alone, century-old frame houses with beautiful yards, stained-glass windows, and circular porches topped with pointy-roofed turrets. Hop on the Q train and check out Ocean Avenue between Newkirk Avenue and Dorchester Road, as well as East 16th, 17th,18th and 19th Streets between Dorchester Road and Ditmas Avenue. You're about to experience a neighborhood with the largest concentration of Victorian-era homes in the USA.

207 DITMAS PARK

208 LITTLE ODESSA

Brighton Beach

For an interesting beach town experience, take the B or Q train to Brighton Beach Avenue and visit the tight-knit Russian-speaking community in Little Odessa a.k.a. Brighton Beach. Named after the Ukrainian city on the Black Sea, it is one of the best places for Russian or Georgian cuisine. Have lunch at Tatiana Grill or Volna, shop for a wide variety of vodkas at any liquor store or go for Russian imports at Brighton Bazaar. Just remember, many shop and restaurant signs are in Cyrillic and the locals often assume you speak Russian.

209 WEBSTER PLACE

Between Prospect Avenue and 16th Street
Park Slope

In the middle of Prospect Avenue and 16 Street (between 6th and 7th Avenues) is a small forgotten street that cuts through the block and is called Webster Place. This sleepy South Slope section displays some of the most tastefully preserved Queen Anne-style homes in Brooklyn. Beautifully painted and conserved, these columned porches and wood-framed houses date back to the late 1860s. There is no record as to who built these remarkable residences, but they remain one of the city's most stunning and hidden collections of houses.

Take a **B O A T** from Brooklyn to...

210 SHEEPSHEAD BAY

Emmons Avenue
Sheepshead Bay

Sheepshead Bay – named after an edible fish found in its waters – is a community that retained its old-school charm, but deep-sea fishing is what you're here for. You can catch fluke, striped bass, porgies, and bluefish by spending a day on one of the many charter boats docked along the famous Emmons Avenue strip. The waters around New York Harbor host a diverse ecosystem due to the warm and cold ocean currents that meet offshore in the New York Bight. Think how cool it would be to go fishing and catch a striped bass in front of Lady Liberty?

211 GOVERNORS ISLAND

Island in New York Harbor ⑥
govisland.com

Should you crave an escape from Brooklyn in the summer, then take the East River Ferry from the Brooklyn Bridge Park Pier 6 / Atlantic Avenue stop to Governors Island. Various fun events take place at this former military base all summer long. A 10-minute ferry ride will bring you to a car-free sanctuary, combining a park, concert venue, adult playground and outdoor art spaces into a lovely haven away from the noisy city.

212 ROCKAWAY BEACH

Queens
nycgovparks.org

To get to Rockaway Beach in Queens, one of New York City's best-kept beach secrets, take the NYC Rockaway Ferry in Sunset Park and from there it's about a 35-minute enjoyable boat ride. Go for tacos, biking, hiking, art galleries but most of all to enjoy a year-round surfer's paradise.

213 JOHN F. KENNEDY INTERNATIONAL AIRPORT

Queens
new.mta.info/ map/7551

Definitely NOT the most practical way to get to JFK, but undeniably an adventurous one. In Sunset Park, take the Rockaway Ferry to Rockaway Beach for a 35-minute scenic boat ride. Once there, walk to Broad Channel Subway Station and hop on the A train to Howard Beach-JFK Airport Subway Station. Then take the AirTrain to whichever terminal you need. Just make sure you have plenty of time and not too much luggage.

214 SANDY HOOK

Middletown, NJ
seastreak.com

Take the South Brooklyn Ferry to Pier 11 / Wall Street and hop on the Seastreak that gets you to some of the best beaches in Sandy Hook, New Jersey, in just 30 minutes. A complimentary shuttle service takes you from the ferry to the various beaches throughout the day. You can also bike the Multi-Use Pathway (MUP), an 8,7-mile (14-kilometer) paved trail that winds its way along the picturesque beaches and historical monuments of this peninsula. For the naturists, head to Gunnison Beach, one of the oldest and best nude beaches on the East Coast. It is a LGBTQ+-friendly spot, too.

215 THE NYC FERRY
ferry.nyc

The fastest and one of the most pleasant ways to get around in New York City is the NYC Ferry. There are six routes, mainly on the East River, which connect 21 ferry piers in the Bronx, Brooklyn, Manhattan, and Queens. The rides offer expansive cityscape views, and the cost is that of a subway ride (2,75 dollar in 2021), with an additional 1 dollar for a bike. Kids under 44 inches (111 centimeters) ride for free when accompanied by an adult.

Highlights of the
GREEN-WOOD CEMETERY

500 25th St
Greenwood Heights ⑦
+1 718 210 3080
green-wood.com

216 ALTAR TO LIBERTY: MINERVA

Battle Hill (a.k.a. Gowan's Heights)

At Battle Hill, the highest point of Brooklyn also known as Gowan's Heights, stands a sculpture of a strong, fearless woman by Frederick Wellington Ruckstull. Minerva, the Roman goddess of arts and war, is her name. She overlooks the site of The Battle of Brooklyn, the first and biggest Revolutionary War combat after the signing of the Declaration of Independence in 1776. Notice how Minerva locks eyes with another legendary woman, the Statue of Liberty, who stands some 3,5 miles (5,6 kilometers) away in New York Harbor.

217 FAMOUS RESIDENTS

Various locations

A few of the famous people buried at Green-Wood are: Jean-Michel Basquiat, the artist; Charles Hercules Ebbets, the owner of the Brooklyn Dodgers; Susan Smith McKinney-Steward, New York's first black physician; Leonard Bernstein, the composer of *West Side Story*; Rev. Henry Ward Beecher, the abolitionist; Samuel Morse, the inventor of the telegraph; and Frank Morgan, the actor who played the *Wizard of Oz*.

218 GREEN-WOOD CHAPEL

Between Landscape and Willow Avenues

The architects responsible for Grand Central Station, Warren and Wetmore, designed this beautiful Gothic-inspired, multifunctional and non-denominational chapel in 1911. It is a reduced copy of Christopher Wren's Thomas Tower at Christ Church College in Oxford, England. With its spare, limestone space, magnificent stained-glass windows, beautiful dome and massive chandelier, Green-Wood Chapel could be the perfect venue for your wedding day. Rental rates start at 1000 dollar for four hours.

219 THE CATACOMBS

Between Locust and Grove Avenues

The catacombs at Green-Wood were built in the 1850s for families who wanted to be laid to rest indoors but couldn't afford mausoleums. These days the catacombs regularly host special events including the classical music concert series *The Angel's Share*. The evening usually starts with a reception at sunset and a whiskey tasting. Guests then wander along winding paths to one of the cemetery's oldest structures for an unusual chamber music performance.

220 THE GATES

25th Street gate
AT: THE MAIN
ENTRANCE AT 500
25TH ST

Fort Hamilton gate
AT: FORT HAMILTON
PARKWAY AND MACIELI
PLACE

The Gothic Revival entry gate at 25th Street was designed by Richard Upjohn & Sons and is constructed of brownstone with sculpted Nova Scotia sandstone panels that feature themes relating to death and resurrection. Make sure to look out for a colony of monk parakeets from Argentina, which nest in the Gothic spire. According to legend they escaped in the 1960s when a crate of caged monk parakeets broke open at JFK airport. The second gate at the Fort Hamilton Parkway entrance consists of the 1876 Caretaker's Residence and the Visitor's Cottage, both excellent examples of the High Victorian Gothic style.

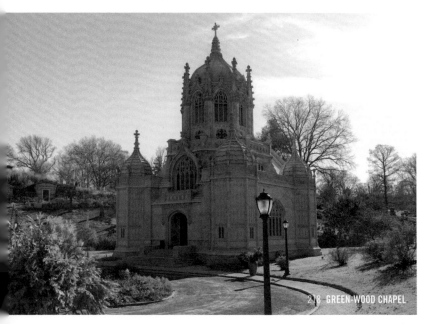

218 GREEN-WOOD CHAPEL

221 SOME OF THE MAUSOLEUMS

Various locations

Steinway Mausoleum: the largest private mausoleum holds the earthly remains of piano makers William and Henry Steinway and some of their family members, and there's room for dozens more.

Niblo Mausoleum: William Niblo was a theater impresario and restaurant owner who built this mausoleum for his wife who died 27 years before him. Up until his death, he regularly hosted parties in front of his mausoleum.

Canda Mausoleum: Charlotte Canda was a debutante who died on the evening of her seventeenth birthday in 1845 in a horse carriage accident in New York City.

Van Ness Parsons Mausoleum: Albert Ross Parsons was a celebrated pianist and music teacher who also was an Egyptologist. So it comes as no surprise that his last resting place is a pyramid.

The SMALLER PARKS
of Brooklyn

222 ADAM YAUCH PARK

27 State St
Brooklyn Heights ④
+1 212 639 9675
nycgovparks.org

This little playground is named after Adam Yauch, a founding member of the hip-hop group the Beastie Boys and a Brooklyn Heights native who died in 2012 at age 47 from cancer. Yauch, better known as MCA, was also an artist, filmmaker and activist. His home borough of Brooklyn was immortalized in the Beastie Boys' 1987 hit *No Sleep Till Brooklyn*.

223 FORT GREENE PARK

100 Washington Park
Fort Greene ④
+1 212 639 9675
fortgreenepark.org

Originally built as Fort Putnam in 1776, Fort Greene Park is Brooklyn's oldest park and was named after Nathanael Greene, a hero of the American Revolutionary War. It is a thriving, lively neighborhood park with rolling hills, open fields, playgrounds, basketball courts and workout areas. Located within the park is the Revolutionary Garden where anything from cucumbers to lettuce and flowers are grown. The park has gardening workshops and some of the products are sold at the Fort Greene Park Greenmarket that takes place every Saturday from 8 am to 3 pm.

224 MANHATTAN BEACH PARK

760 Oriental
Boulevard
Manhattan Beach ®
+1 212 639 9675
nycgovparks.org

Bring your picnic basket and set up a barbecue along the water at this small, family-friendly beach park which is a little calmer than neighboring Brighton Beach. Manhattan Beach Park has playgrounds, two large baseball diamonds, as well as tennis, volleyball, basketball and handball fields. This park has plenty of room for all types of active outdoor fun.

225 MSGR. MCGOLRICK PARK

Russell St, Monitor
St, between
Nassau and Driggs
Avenues
Greenpoint ①
+1 212 639 9675
nycgovparks.org

Msgr. McGolrick Park offers visitors a quieter and more relaxed experience than its busy neighbor, McCarren Park. It is low-key, dog-friendly, and filled with large old trees that provide plenty of shade during the summer. The gated play area has swings, spray showers, and creative climbing structures for kids of all ages. There are two monuments in the park: The World War I memorial (1923), designed by Carl Augustus Heber, and *The Monitor and the Merrimac* (1939) by sculptor Antonio de Filippo.

226 OWL'S HEAD PARK

Colonial Road, 68
St and Shore Road
Bay Ridge ®
+1 212 639 9675
nycgovparks.org

This small park in Bay Ridge has 24 pleasant acres of woods, hills, playgrounds, huge basketball courts, windy pathways by the water, breathtaking views and a skating ramp. It is also home to some of the most beautiful and unique trees in Brooklyn. Make sure to also check out the nearby American Veterans Memorial Pier with the *Beacon*, a Brooklyn Remembers 9/11 Memorial, designed and built by the artist Robert Ressler.

227 SUNSET PARK

41 St, 44 St,
between 5th and
7th Avenues
Sunset Park ⑦
+1 212 639 9675
nycgovparks.org

In summer, Sunset Park and its public outdoor pool become home to swimmers and sun worshipers from all over Brooklyn. The Olympic-sized pool, which opened its waters to the public in 1936, was built in a neoclassical/art deco-style by Aymar Embury II. In 2007, the interior and exterior received city landmark designation. Note that admission is free to all NYC public pools.

Interesting **NATURE** spots

228 CANARSIE PIER

Canarsie ⑧
+1 718 338 3799
nyharborparks.org

On the very south end of Rockaway Parkway you'll find Canarsie Pier, an old restored fishing pier. Fun things to do there include kayaking with ranger-led trips to nearby Canarsie Pol – an uninhabited island south of Canarsie –, picnicking and barbequing, summer concerts and, of course, lots of fishing.

229 LONG MEADOW AND THE RAVINE

95 Prospect
Park West
Prospect Park ⑦
+1 718 965 8951
*prospectpark.org/
visit-the-park*

Designed by the same architects as Central Park, Prospect Park is Brooklyn's second largest park and has some interesting nature spots. The Long Meadow, possibly the longest unbroken meadow in any urban US park, spans almost a mile (1,6 kilometer) of open green space and is a popular spot for countless summertime activities. The Ravine, located between the Long Meadow and the Nethermead, is Brooklyn's only real forest, and is home to some of the park's oldest trees. It extends along a gushing stream, a lush pool – often visited by mallards or herons – and a scenic waterfall.

230 GLASS BOTTLE BEACH AT DEAD HORSE BAY

RYAN VISITOR CENTER
1 Floyd Bennett Field
Barren Island ⑧
+1 718 338 3799
nps.gov/gate/learn/
historyculture/ryan-
visitor-center

Sadly, in August 2020, Dead Horse Bay near Jamaica Bay in South Brooklyn was closed after radioactive waste was found, and now the beach is being cleaned up. We do want to mention this interesting spot, given its very peculiar history. Dead Horse Bay got its name in the 1850s when horse-rendering plants surrounded the beach. In the 1950s, a landfill connected the island to the mainland but, for reasons unknown, the trash wasn't properly covered and debris started to escape. Since then, thousands of bottles, cutlery and dishes, floor tiles, tons of shoes, and more could be found along the beach. It was trash, but a fascinating place to observe years of NYC history, and a scavenger's paradise. The path to the beach can be overgrown, so sturdy shoes and insect repellent are highly recommended. Be warned, this is not a beach for children!

231 NORTH FORTY NATURAL AREA

AT: FLOYD BENNETT FIELD
Barren Island ⑧
+1 718 338 3799
nyharborparks.org

The North Forty Natural Area is located in the northernmost corner of Floyd Bennett Field in Jamaica Bay. It has hiking trails and a man-made freshwater pond called Return-a-Gift Pond, with bird blinds so you can observe birds and other wildlife without disturbing them. During the summer breeding season you can spot waterfowl here, such as wood ducks, northern shovelers and green-winged teal, as well as the great blue heron and black-crowned night-heron.

232 JAMAICA BAY WILDLIFE REFUGE BROOKLYN

175-10 Cross Bay
Boulevard
Queens NY 11693 ⑧
+1 718 318 4340
nyharborparks.org

The Jamaica Bay Wildlife Refuge, west of JFK in both Brooklyn and Queens, consists of numerous islands, a labyrinth of waterways, meadowlands, and two freshwater ponds. It is one of the most significant wild birds and other native species sanctuaries in the northeastern USA, and one of the best places in NYC to observe migrating species. With 332 bird species sighted over the past 25 years, it is a birder's paradise. You can take classes on seasonal wildlife, sunset tours, hikes, boat trips, and more. But just sitting on a bench in that beautiful nature and seeing Manhattan rise up like Oz in the distance is pretty spectacular too. You can just imagine what a pre-industrialized New York would have been like.

233 MARINE PARK HIKING TRAILS

Fillmore Ave
Marine Park ⑧
+1 212 639 9675
*nycgovparks.org/
parks/marine-park*

Marine Park, an urban oasis along the shoreline, is Brooklyn's largest public park. The park has a 530-acre (2,15-square-kilometer) salt marsh and grassland nature preserve, and its well-groomed hiking trails offer a chance to experience this fragile ecosystem up close, and make you feel like you're very far away from the hustle and bustle of Brooklyn. It's worth noting that you're surrounded by one of the busiest residential neighborhoods in Brooklyn.

Best spots to stare at the
MANHATTAN SKYLINE

234 BROOKLYN BRIDGE PARK – PIER 1

2 Furman St
Brooklyn Bridge
Park ③
+1 718 222 9939
brooklynbridge
park.org

There is a good reason why Pier 1 in Brooklyn Bridge Park is one of the most popular places for wedding pictures. Few places in NYC offer a more iconic skyline view of the city. Enjoy the New York Harbor from the granite steps – built from stones salvaged from the Roosevelt Island Bridge reconstruction –, lay on one of the three magnificent lawns for an amazing panoramic view of lower Manhattan, or plop yourself down on a bench on the waterfront promenade for a unique waterfront experience and watch the sunset.

235 EAST RIVER STATE PARK (MARSHA P. JOHNSON STATE PARK)

90 Kent Avenue
Williamsburg ①
+1 718 782 2731
parks.ny.gov/parks

For an unobstructed view of Midtown Manhattan and the Williamsburg Bridge head to the concrete-heavy East River State Park, renamed the Marsha P. Johnson State Park (Marsha P. Johnson was a transgender woman of color who was a pioneer of the LGBTQ civil rights movement) in February 2020. Apart from the magnificent city vistas, the eclectic food market Smorgasburg sets up shop here on Saturdays from April through October with 100 local vendors, attracting 20.000 to 30.000 people every weekend.

237 MAIN STREET PARK

238 LOUIS VALENTINO JR. PARK AND PIER

236 WNYC TRANSMITTER PARK

West St, between
Greenpoint Avenue
and Kent St
Greenpoint ⓘ
+1 212 639 9675
nycgovparks.org

This relatively small and new – it opened in 2012 – park is a waterfront destination located along the East River in Greenpoint. Explore natural wetland landscaping, a nautically themed children's play area, a pedestrian bridge and a pier with gorgeous views of Manhattan. Don't miss the beautiful and very instagrammable mural of a girl with flowers, *Love Me, Love Me Not,* by FAILE, the Brooklyn-based artistic collaboration between Patrick McNeil and Patrick Miller.

237 MAIN STREET PARK

NEXT TO: EMPIRE
FULTON FERRY
Dumbo ③
+1 718 222 9939
brooklynbridge
park.org

Take a seat on the curving stone bleachers at popular Pebble Beach in the Dumbo section of Brooklyn Bridge Park and enjoy the views of Lower Manhattan and the Brooklyn Bridge. The park also has a nautically themed playground, an expanded and elevated lawn, a dog run, and the largest outdoor rock-climbing facility in North America.

238 LOUIS VALENTINO JR. PARK AND PIER

Ferris St, between
Coffey St and
Van Dyke St
Red Hook ⑥
+1 212 639 9675
nycgovparks.org/
parks/valentino-pier

Tucked away in Red Hook, the Louis Valentino Jr. Park and Pier is a relatively unknown leisure spot that is typically occupied by local picnickers, fishermen, and Red Hook hipsters. Watch the Staten Island Ferry sail by, enjoy the panoramic views of the Manhattan Harbor and skyline, but, most importantly, take in the city's best and closest front-facing view of the Statue of Liberty.

Find Brooklyn's best
URBAN FARMS

239 BROOKLYN GRANGE

**63 Flushing
Avenue
Brooklyn Navy
Yard ③
+1 347 670 3660
*brooklyngrange
farm.com***

The 5,6-acre (25.000-square-meter) organic urban rooftop farm that grows vegetables and honey for local restaurants, markets, and community-supported agriculture is located on three rooftops in Brooklyn and Queens. The two farms in Brooklyn are at Navy Yard and Sunset Park. All locations offer guided tours by friendly and knowledgeable staff, workshops on food, farming, wellness, sustainability, business, and beyond, as well as farm dinners by famous chefs, and sunset yoga on the roof.

240 GOTHAM GREENS

WHOLE FOODS MARKET
**214 3rd St
Gowanus ⑥
+1 718 935 0600
*gothamgreens.com***

Gotham Greens' sustainable greenhouses are sun (and wind) powered and climate controlled for year-round growing. From an observation deck just outside The Cafe at Food Bazaar, you can observe a wall of windows and an expanse of greens that spans 20.000 square feet (6096 square meters). The lettuces and herbs are gathered and delivered to fine restaurants and grocers across town. They offer free tours during which you can learn about their process as well as get a chance to try the product.

241 RED HOOK COMMUNITY FARM

560 Columbia St
Red Hook ⑥
+1 718 858 6782
rhicenter.org/red-hook-farms/the-farms

This community farm is one of Brooklyn's largest located on what used to be a concrete baseball field. It is run by Added Value, a nonprofit that trains teens in the logistics of urban agriculture, from planting seeds to making compost and selling the food. Over 15.000 pounds (6800 kilos) of produce are harvested each year, and hundreds of volunteers and host community events are welcomed throughout the growing season. Local restaurants and residents buy the farm's produce – more than 30 crops in all, including arugula, beets, okra, heirloom tomatoes, chard, beans, garlic and basil, as well as cut flowers.

242 ROOFTOP REDS

299 Sands St, building 275
Brooklyn Navy Yard ③
+1 917 284 9254
rooftopreds.com

Sitting on top a converted factory building in the newly renovated Brooklyn Navy Yard, Rooftop Reds serves red wine as well as white and rosé as well. The tables are arranged under row upon row of vines growing in planters, that have been specially devised for rooftop viticulture. With views of Downtown Brooklyn and with Sea Planes circling overhead on approach to land in the East River, it's a world unto its own. The vines only yield one barrel of wine a year, which explains why the majority of the wines on offer is from the NY Finger Lakes. The rooftop grown wine is available, but it's a precious commodity and sold by the ounce. The Navy Yard is serviced by all forms of transportation as well as the NYC Ferry but it's a big 300-acre (1,2-square-kilometer) complex so be prepared for a bit of a walk depending on where you enter. Once there, you'll step into another world, full of wine, conversation, and pizza ordered from a local delivery and brought right to your table.

Some great **HOLISTIC HEALTH** *spots*

243 **ELEMENT NATURAL HEALING ARTS**

518 Henry St
Carroll Gardens ⑥
+1 718 855 4850
elementhealing.com

The services offered at Element Natural Healing Arts are vast: acupuncture, massage, facials, skincare, waxing, cupping, reflexology, lymphatic drainage, infrared sauna, herbs, supplements, and nutrition services. Basically everything you are looking for to improve your health and well-being. Licensed acupuncturists and Oriental Medicine diplomat Christina Morris opened the space in 2001 while working at a hospital in New York. While some services are more inclined to pampering – the deep-cleansing facial, the relaxing, oil-massaging scalp treatment – Element is known for its skills in treating injuries, abating chronic pains like migraines, and finding natural solutions to illnesses like diabetes. The precautions they have put in place to keep clients, patients, and employees safe are just as comprehensive.

244 PROGRESSIVE PILATES WILLIAMSBURG

169 Wythe Avenue
Williamsburg ①
+1 718 755 8606
progressivepilates
williamsburg.com

It is said that Progressive Pilates Williamsburg has the best Pilates classes in Brooklyn. If you want to understand your body better, the experienced staff here will definitely help you. They are trained in a variety of methods, from Alexander technique and Thai yoga bodywork to reflexology, giving them a unique understanding of how to teach biomechanical movement and postural alignment. Several sessions in, you'll feel stronger in body and calmer in mind.

245 SLOPE WELLNESS

816 8th Avenue
Park Slope ⑦
+1 718 415 0738
slopewellnessny.com

Slope Wellness's mission is to deliver the highest quality treatments and customer care to those seeking holistic and natural healthcare. On offer are acupuncture, massage, herbology, and skin care with a comprehensive and integrative approach. Their extensive team works together with the clients and patients to find the most appropriate practitioners and services to help them achieve their health and wellness goals. They give a discount to patients whose insurance doesn't cover acupuncture.

246 STUDIO MAYA

603 Bergen St
Prospect Heights ⑤
+1 917 837 3705
studiomaya.com

Maya Jocelyn, a former dancer, opened her space in 2008 after an avalanche of injuries and chronic back pain. In a beautiful tranquil studio, she teaches a unique technique called JATi which turns your core to be the power center of your body and supports your recovery from chronic pain and injuries. During the pandemic Maya switched entirely to virtual classes which are followed by people from all over the world.

STEINBERG FAMILY SCULPTURE GARDEN

CULTURE Ⓐ

The top commercial
ART GALLERIES

247 CLEARING

**396 Johnson
Avenue
East Williams-
burg** ②
+1 718 456 0396
c-l-e-a-r-i-n-g.com

This sleek, spacious contemporary art gallery located in a former truck repair depot in Bushwick was founded by Belgian artist Olivier Babin in 2010. Their second space opened in Brussels in 2012, and in 2017 they launched a public showroom in Manhattan. With a focus on young contemporary artists – a number of them had their very first show at the gallery – the gallery now represents some of the most in-demand new talent like Korakrit Arunanondchai, Marina Pinsky, Calvin Marcus, and Harold Ancart.

248 TRANSMITTER

**1329 Willoughby
Avenue
Bushwick** ②
+1 646 389 9407
transmitter.nyc

The artist-run space Transmitter focuses on multidisciplinary, international, and experimental programming. Exhibitions are diverse in terms of content, and show both underrepresented artists and established artists, both local and abroad. They also organize artist talks, screenings, panel discussions, readings, and performances. Also check out the independently operated, artist-run Tiger Strikes Asteroid, which shares the space and has branches across the country.

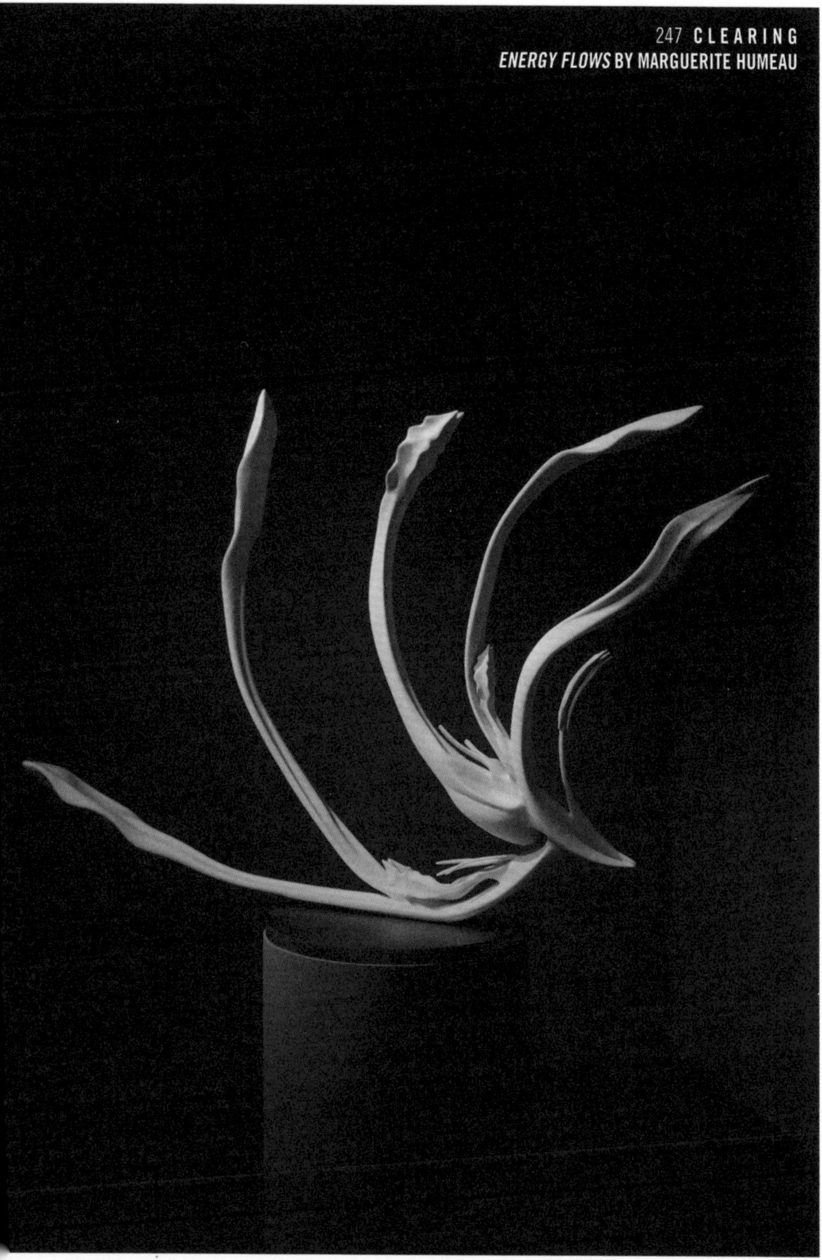

247 **CLEARING**
ENERGY FLOWS BY MARGUERITE HUMEAU

249 LUHRING AUGUSTINE BUSHWICK

**25 Knickerbocker Avenue
East Williams-burg** ②
+1 718 386 2746
luhringaugustine.com

Founded in 1985 by co-owners Lawrence Luhring and Roland Augustine, Luhring Augustine is a mainstay of Chelsea, and also opened an additional 3500 square-foot (1066-square-meter) space in TriBeCa, in Manhattan. The gallery uses its Bushwick space for wide-ranging and interesting projects. The building is an open, flexible exhibition space that can accommodate large-scale installations, film and video, and long-term projects. Their recent historic exhibition brings together artists from the gallery in dialogue with the façade of a 19th-century Indian pleasure pavilion. Luhring Augustine represents important internationally known artists like Christopher Wool, Rachel Whiteread, and Pipilotti Rist.

250 MICROSCOPE GALLERY

**1329 Willoughby Avenue
Bushwick** ②
+1 347 925 1433
microscope gallery.com

The artists and curators Elle Burchill and Andrea Monti established Microscope Gallery in 2010 to present works from artists in all mediums with an emphasis on moving image, performance, digital art and photography. In 2011, performance artist Marni Kotak transformed Microscope Gallery into a provisional maternity ward and gave birth to Baby X as a performance (*The Birth of Baby X*), blurring the lines between 'real life' and the aesthetic object. Other artists represented by the gallery are Katherine Bauer, Zach Nader, and Peggy Ahwesh. Microscope Gallery is also known for showing works of such pioneering figures as Jonas Mekas, the godfather of American avant-garde cinema. Sadly, Microscope recently relocated to 525 W 29th Street in Manhattan.

251 MINUS SPACE

16 Main St
Dumbo ③
+1 718 801 8095
minusspace.com

Minus Space, a lovely street-level gallery in Dumbo, presents contemporary reductive abstract art – an artistic style or an aesthetic, rather than an art movement. Matthew Deleget and Rossana Martinez, both exhibiting artists, started the gallery as an online forum in 2003 and now the gallery presents solo and group exhibitions of pioneering emerging and established artists. During the 2020 pandemic, Minus Space launched an online bookstore featuring new and vintage publications by the gallery and affiliated artists. The gallery values Land Recognition, and mention that it is located in Lenapehoking, the homeland of the Lenape peoples. They respectfully acknowledge their past and present cultural and spiritual connection to this area.

252 STUDIO 10

56 Bogart St
East Williams-
burg ②
+1 718 852 4396
studio10bogart.com

One of the original hubs of this neighborhood's art scene; 56 Bogart Street is teaming with artists, studios and workshops. The main floor houses a wide variety of galleries. Don't miss Studio 10, founded by Larry Greenberg with the idea of presenting a free form exhibition venue crossing many practices. Studio 10 presents performance, painting and installation from a wide multi-generational community of artists. The only criterion is that the work needs to engage Larry.

Cool nonprofit
ARTS ORGANIZATIONS

253 **A.I.R. GALLERY**
   155 Plymouth St
   Dumbo ③
   +1 212 255 6651
   airgallery.org

The first all-women artist-directed art gallery in the USA, A.I.R. Gallery was founded in SoHo in 1972 by women in support of female artists. A.I.R. Gallery moved to Dumbo in 2008 and is still going strong, exhibiting the work of hundreds of women each year. They also host events, lectures and symposia on feminism, art and so much more.

254 **BRIC**
   647 Fulton St
   Fort Greene ④
   +1 718 683 5600
   bricartsmedia.org

BRIC is a leading arts and media institution whose work spans contemporary visual and performing arts, media, and civic action. They are the leading presenter of free cultural programming in Brooklyn. The BRIC House in Fort Greene offers a public media center, a major contemporary art exhibition space, two performance spaces, a glass-walled TV studio, and artist work spaces. They also organize the BRIC Celebrate Brooklyn! Festival in Prospect Park.

255 EYEBEAM

185 Wythe Ave,
Office F1
Bushwick ②
+1 347 378 9163
eyebeam.org

Eyebeam, a platform for artists to engage creatively with technology in an experimental setting, believes that artists can help us visualize and realize a more just future. In the spring of 2020, amidst a global pandemic and international protests, Eyebeam was forced to put its flagship residency program on hold and closed its physical space. In response, it launched a new artist-led initiative called Rapid Response for a Better Digital Future and asked artists to carve out a path towards a more humane vision for the future.

256 MOCADA

80 Hanson Place
Fort Greene ④
+1 718 230 0492
mocada.org

In 2017, the Museum of Contemporary African Diasporan Arts moved into a new building in Fort Greene that also houses four BAM Cinema theatres, a branch of the Brooklyn Public Library and 651 ARTS, a Brooklyn-based arts presenter of theater, dance and music grounded in the African Diaspora. MoCADA's mission has always been to build community through art, both locally and globally, and to stimulate dialogue on pressing social and political issues facing the African Diaspora. There's a great gift shop, too, offering a unique selection of products by contemporary designers, artisans and authors.

257 PIONEER WORKS

159 Pioneer St
Red Hook ⑥
+1 718 596 3001
pioneerworks.org

This beautiful three-story red brick, former iron-works-factory on Pioneer Street has been the home for Pioneer Works since 2012. Founded by artist Dustin Yellin, this artist-run cultural center wants to build communities through art, tech, music and science. The building accommodates a recording studio, a media lab, a darkroom, 3D printers, artist studios, galleries, gardens, and a bookshop. The central hall is home to a rotating schedule of cool art exhibitions, interesting science talks, music performances, workshops, and innovative free public programming. As they undergo their first major renovation, they have temporarily relocated to Red Hook Labs at 133 Imlay Street. The renovated building will reopen in the spring of 2022.

258 SMACK MELLON

92 Plymouth St
Dumbo ③
+1 718 834 8761
smackmellon.org

Since 1995, Smack Mellon offers emerging artists support and recognition, providing a space for creation, exploration and exhibitions outside the commercial art world. Smack Mellon's Artist Studio Program provides free studio space, access to a fabrication workshop, a media lab with editing suites, and a fellowship to six artists for a yearlong residency.

Hipster CONCERT HALLS

259 BROOKLYN BOWL
61 Wythe Avenue
Williamsburg ①
+1 718 963 3369
brooklynbowl.com

Brooklyn Bowl is an 800-capacity music venue, a sixteen-lane bowling alley, and a traditional American restaurant operated by the popular citywide chain Blue Ribbon. The bars serve only draught beers brewed within Brooklyn. Fun fact: Bill Clinton held a fundraiser for his wife Hillary Clinton for the 2016 Presidency at Brooklyn Bowl.

260 BROOKLYN STEEL
319 Frost St
East Williams-
burg ①
+1 888 929 7849
bowerypresents.com

Named one of the 10 best live music venues in the USA by *Rolling Stone Magazine*, this warehouse-turned-live music venue can hold 800 music lovers and has welcomed the likes of LCD Soundsystem, PJ Harvey, Goldfrapp, Pixies, and Arctic Monkeys. This former steel fabrication shop has an impressive speaker system and great sight lines that allows for a wide range of genres to shine.

261 KINGS THEATRE
1027 Flatbush
Avenue
Flatbush ②
+1 718 856 5464
kingstheatre.com

This magnificent old vaudeville and movie palace opened as Loew's Kings Theatre in 1929. Following World War II, it steadily deteriorated until it officially closed in 1977. After a 95-million-dollar renovation, this state-of-the-art live performance venue reopened with meticulously restored plaster moldings, pink marble staircases, a honeycomb ceiling and an inaugural performance by Diana Ross in 2015.

259 BROOKLYN BOWL

261 KINGS THEATRE

262 KNITTING FACTORY

361 Metropolitan Avenue
Williamsburg ⓘ
+1 347 529 6696
knittingfactory.com

This historic Knitting Factory opened as an experimental-noise sanctuary in 1987 on Houston Street in Manhattan. It relocated to TriBeCa in 1994 and slowly transformed into a more accessible concert hall, until they made a move to Williamsburg in 2009. There are two rooms: The Front Room, an airy bar area, with glass-front walls, big, cushy booths, and a large window into The Venue, the intimate and charming back, where the shows actually go on. The programming is a combination of small-stakes indie rock, comedy, underground hip-hop, and oddball one-off events.

263 MUSIC HALL OF WILLIAMSBURG

66 N 6th St
Williamsburg ⓘ
+1 718 486 5400
musichallof williamsburg.com

A short walk from the L train is the smaller music venue Music Hall of Williamsburg – it has a capacity of 550 people – that is operated by The Bowery Presents. The programming is indie rock, underground, cutting-edge or avant-garde rock concerts. It was there – when still called Northsix – that indie musician and multi-instrumentalist Elliott Smith performed live for the last time before his untimely death in 2003.

264 WARSAW

261 Driggs Avenue
Greenpoint ⓘ
+1 212 777 6800
warsawconcerts.com

Located inside the Polish National Home in the heart of Greenpoint, the unassuming Warsaw, a 1000-capacity music club, is a local favorite and industry go-to for punk bands, hip-hop artists, DJs, and more. Or as they describe it "It's a venue where Pierogies meet Punk!", and you can actually eat pierogies there.

A

Some of the best
PERFORMANCE SPACES

265 **BARGEMUSIC**
AT: FULTON FERRY
LANDING
1 Water St
Brooklyn Bridge
Park ③
+1 718 624 4924
bargemusic.org

Situated near the base of the Brooklyn Bridge at Fulton Ferry Landing, Bargemusic is a 19th-century converted coffee barge that has been presenting classical chamber music for more than four decades. The 102-foot-long (31-meter-long) boat, built in 1899, hosts about two hundred performances each year. The experience of great live music in an intimate wood-paneled room with excellent acoustics and views of Lower Manhattan is a must-do.

266 **BROOKLYN ACADEMY OF MUSIC (BAM)**
30 Lafayette Avenue
Fort Greene ④
+1 718 636 4100
bam.org

The Brooklyn Academy of Music is a true Brooklyn institution and America's oldest performing arts center. It has presented the most innovative talents in theater, dance, music, film and literature since 1861. BAM showcases the work of emerging artists and innovative modern masters. Its hottest ticket is its signature Next Wave Festival, an international showcase for cutting-edge performance. There is also BAMcinématek that presents film classics, festivals, premieres and retrospectives, and Dance-Africa, the nation's largest festival dedicated to African and African-diasporic dance, performance, art and film.

267 NATIONAL SAWDUST

80 N 6th St
Williamsburg ⓘ
+1 646 779 8455
nationalsawdust.org

National Sawdust is both a state-of-the-art performance venue and a recording studio housed within a preserved century-old sawdust factory, which has won multiple architecture awards. The focus is on discovery within music: they introduce audiences to new artists and styles and artists to new audiences. The organization gives composers and musicians resources, time and space to develop their art, as well as support for project development and realization.

266 BROOKLYN ACADEMY OF MUSIC (BAM)

268 ROULETTE

**509 Atlantic
Avenue
Boerum Hill** ④
+1 917 267 0368
roulette.org

Roulette was founded in a loft on West Broadway in TriBeCa in 1978 to present experimental art by artists like John Cage, Philip Glass, and Meredith Monk. It is now an internationally recognized center for musical innovation based in Downtown Brooklyn. Their programming has expanded globally through Roulette's online and television broadcast programs where audiences all over the world can explore the treasures of their archives.

269 ST. ANN'S WAREHOUSE

AT: BROOKLYN
BRIDGE PARK
**45 Water St
Dumbo** ③
+1 718 254 8779
stannswarehouse.org

Housed within the walls of the original 1860 Tobacco Warehouse in Dumbo, St. Ann's Warehouse is a multi-disciplinary venue that has been presenting avant-garde theater and concerts for almost four decades. The new building includes a large, versatile theater space, with capacity for 300 to 700 people, to accommodate St. Ann's core theater and music programming, a studio for smaller-scale events and community uses, as well as The Max Family Garden, which is open to Brooklyn Bridge Park visitors.

Ⓐ

Great MUSIC FESTIVALS
in Brooklyn

270 BRIC CELEBRATE BROOKLYN! FESTIVAL

AT: PROSPECT PARK BANDSHELL

141 Prospect Park West
Prospect Park ⑦
+1 718 683 5600
bricartsmedia.org

The BRIC Celebrate Brooklyn! Festival is one of New York City's longest running, free, outdoor performing arts festivals. More than 250.000 attendees from across NYC gather at the Prospect Park Bandshell each summer to see talent from around the world. Performers who have appeared at the festival include: They Might Be Giants, The Neville Brothers, Ladysmith Black Mambazo, Angelique Kidjo, Amadou & Mariam, Dr. John, Joan Armatrading and Hugh Masekela.

271 AFROPUNK FEST

AT: COMMODORE BARRY PARK

Flushing Avenue and N. Elliot Place
Fort Greene ④
afropunk.com

Debuting at the BAM in 2005, Afropunk is a three-day eclectic extravaganza in Fort Greene with music, activism, fashion and art, celebrating Black and African culture with a punk attitude. Head to Commodore Barry Park at the end of August to enjoy an impressive line-up of African Americans and other Black alternative acts. The festival has recently expanded to Atlanta, Paris, London and Johannesburg.

272 BROOKLYN FOLK FESTIVAL

AT: ST. ANN'S CHURCH
157 Montague St
Brooklyn Heights ④
+1 718 395 3214
brooklynfolkfest.com

The three-day Brooklyn Folk Festival is held annually at the gorgeous historic St. Ann's Church in Brooklyn Heights. It includes 30+ bands, vocal and instrumental workshops, a family-friendly square dance, jam sessions, film screenings, the famous Banjo Toss contest, and more. It is presented by the Jalopy Theatre & School of Music, a grassroots community space that is a music venue, music school, instrument store and record label.

A

@BRIANWOODEN
@THEBUSHWICKCOLLECTIVE

Cool **C R E A T I V E** *initiatives*

---

273 **BROOKLYN ART LIBRARY**
28 Frost St
Williamsburg ①
+1 718 388 7941
brooklynart library.org

The Brooklyn Art Library houses the Sketchbook Project: a collaborative library of artists' sketchbooks that has grown every year since 2006. It's basically a free museum where you can touch the art. The Library is home to over 41.000 sketchbooks from artists over 130 different countries. All of these sketchbooks are available to check out in the library for free, and many sketches from the project are now also available digitally on the Brooklyn Art Library website.

274 **THE BUSHWICK COLLECTIVE**
Bushwick ②
thebushwick collective.com

The brainchild of Bushwick native Joe Ficalora, The Bushwick Collective, is NYC's most prolific open-air gallery for street art and graffiti since the first mural appeared in 2011. The ever-expanding Collective has transformed its neighborhood from a largely grim industrial district into a vibrant tourist destination. Their Block Party is an annual event that combines graffiti, street art, music, food trucks and local vendors. The Collective brings together the best of the community and it is a testament to the power of art to transform a neighborhood.

A

275 **INTERNATIONAL STUDIO & CURATORIAL PROGRAM (ISCP)**

1040 Metropolitan Avenue
East Williamsburg ①
+1 718 387 2900
iscp-nyc.org

With 35 light-filled work studios and two galleries, ISCP is New York's most comprehensive international visual arts residency program, founded in 1994. More than 1700 artists and curators from more than 85 countries have undertaken residencies at ISCP. Housed in a former factory, ISCP organizes exhibitions, events and off-site projects, which are free and open to all.

276 **NITEHAWK CINEMA**

188 Prospect Park West
Prospect Park ⑦
+1 646 963 9295
nitehawkcinema.com

This one-of-a-kind independent movie house offers in-seat table-service of gourmet concessions using products from Brooklyn artisans while watching a nicely curated movie selection. This location is one of the oldest buildings in New York that has continuously housed a movie theater, which originally opened in August 1928 as The Sanders Theatre. Occasionally, they serve specialty items and cocktails that are inspired by individual films. Their other location is in Williamsburg.

277 **SYNDICATED BAR-THEATER-KITCHEN**

40 Bogart St
East Williamsburg ②
+1 718 386 3399
syndicatedbk.com

This dine-in movie theater hosts film screenings, often curated according to director or themes, and serves American food like burgers, sandwiches and tater tots, along with cocktails and seasonal beers. Separate from the dining area is a 50-seat screening room that has its own menu. Their Sidewalk Cinema, located on the Thames Street side of the building, is a fun first-come, first-served outdoor cinema and dining area.

278 THE LOT RADIO

17 Nassau Avenue
Williamsburg ⓘ
+1 347 292 7749
thelotradio.com

When Belgian expat Francois Vaxelaire stumbled upon a triangular patch of land in Williamsburg, he had the brilliant idea to create an independent online radio station here, with 24/7 live video streaming from a reclaimed shipping container. There's a lovely outside area where beer, wine, coffee and pastries are served, accompanied by some of the best music across all styles New York City has to offer.

Best things to see at the
BROOKLYN MUSEUM

200 Eastern Parkway
Prospect Heights ⑤
+1 718 638 5000
brooklynmuseum.org

279 ARTS OF AFRICA
**Throughout
the museum**

The Brooklyn Museum was one of the first museums in the USA to collect and exhibit arts of Africa. The collection of approximately 4500 works focuses primarily on historical works from Western, Central, Southern and Eastern Africa, and includes contemporary art from across the continent. This is where African and African Diaspora communities connect with their histories, and where everyone can connect with African cultures. It is where some great artists – Romare Bearden, Jack Whitten, Jean-Michel Basquiat, and others – found inspiration, and where young artists continue to be inspired.

280 NAPOLEON LEADING THE ARMY OVER THE ALPS (2005)

BY KEHINDE WILEY

Martha A. and Robert S. Rubin Pavilion, 1st Fl.

Kehinde Wiley, the art star who gained fame for his portrait of President Obama in 2017, has an older work, called *Napoleon Leading the Army over the Alps*, in the Brooklyn Museum that dates from 2005. It depicts an equestrian portrait of a youthful black male mimicking the posture of the figure of Napoleon Bonaparte in Jacques-Louis David's painting. In 2019, Wiley opened a multidisciplinary artist-in-residence in Dakar to bring together visual artists, writers and filmmakers to live and work together.

280 NAPOLEAN LEADING THE ARMY OVER THE ALPS

281 STEINBERG FAMILY SCULPTURE GARDEN

Steinberg Family Sculpture Garden, 1st Fl.

Created in 1966, this sculpture garden displays a beautiful collection of terracotta, limestone, brownstone, granite, or marble architectural statues rescued from New York City demolition sites. Much of the work was executed by anonymous stone carvers – mostly immigrant workers from the United Kingdom and Italy – who traveled from building site to building site between 1880 and 1910.

281 STEINBERG FAMILY SCULPTURE GARDEN

282 THE DINNER PARTY (1974–79)
BY JUDY CHICAGO
Elizabeth A. Sackler Center for Feminist Art, 4th Fl.

The Dinner Party by Judy Chicago – a work that was five years in the making (1974-1979) – is a wonderful tribute to women and the product of the volunteer labor of more than 400 people. It's a must see and a testament to the power of feminist vision and artistic collaborations. When first shown in San Francisco in 1979, it was not regarded as a work of art but a piece of clumsy political rhetoric. Now, it is considered a key work of contemporary art and is one of the most famous feminist artworks of all time.

283 JAN MARTENSE SCHENCK HOUSE (1676)
Decorative Arts, Schenck Gallery, 4th Fl.

This little house gives you a good idea of how prosperous Dutch families used to live in colonial English Flatlands in Brooklyn. It is a reconstruction based on careful analysis of the original surviving elements of the house, as well as other surviving Dutch Colonial houses. For a long period after about 1730, the two-room core of the house changed very little, and therefore the curators chose this moment in the early 18th century to interpret this house. Too bad that none of the original furniture owned by the Schencks is known to have survived.

284 THE MUMMY CHAMBER
Egyptian Art Galleries, 3rd Fl.

In the Mummy Chamber, the museum uses ancient Egyptian artifacts in order to showcase the ancient practice of mummification. More than 170 items are on display including human and animal mummies, coffins, canopic jars, burial goods and jewelry. There is the mummy of the priest Thothirdes, the mummy of Hor, and a nearly 25-foot-long (7,62-meter-long) *Book of the Dead* scroll.

A

DOMINO PARK

CHILDREN

Take your kids on an **ADVENTURE**

285 BROOKLYN BOULDERS

575 Degraw St
Gowanus ⑥
+1 347 834 9066
brooklyn
boulders.com/
gowanus

For everyone, young and old, who is feeling a bit adventurous and wants to do some rock climbing, this massive, technicolored climbing space was created with you in mind. Located in Gowanus – easy to get to by train to the Atlantic Avenue-Barclays Center stop – it has 10.000 square feet (3048 square meters) of bouldering, auto-belay, top rope, and lead climbing, as well as a section with a yoga studio and gym equipment. If you are a beginner they offer classes for all skill levels and ages. Additionally, all the locals who come here are always friendly and welcoming to new faces.

286 HALLOWEEN IN THE HEIGHTS

Brooklyn Heights ④

It's hard to find more cheerful blocks in the Heights than Garden Place and Grace Court Alley – closed off for traffic in honor of the holiday – where residents make an enormous effort. They construct elaborate Halloween displays in front of their historic brownstones with fake coffins, life-size mummies, smoke machines, and more. Kids are dressed up in the most imaginative costumes. It's all a lot of fun. Try to go early if you want to leave with lots of treats in your bucket!

287 DOMINO PARK

300 Kent Avenue
Williamsburg ①
+1 212 484 2700
dominopark.com

Domino Park – five acres (two square kilometers) of absolute wonder – is located along the Williamsburg waterfront north of the Williamsburg bridge. It was developed on the site of the old Domino Sugar Refinery – once the largest sugar refinery in the world – and features an elevated walkway, plenty of picnic grass, a dog run, bocce ball, beach volleyball, and a playground which is one of the most striking and innovative playgrounds in NYC. Its main attractions are the Sugarcube Centrifuge, a Sugar Cane Cabin and the Sweetwater Silo. These three primary structures were designed by Brooklyn-based artist Mark Reigelman to resemble the sugar factory and feature reclaimed wood and aluminum molds from salvage wheels, all from the Domino factory.

288 OLD STONE HOUSE

336 3rd St
Park Slope ⑥
+1 718 768 3195
theoldstonehouse.org

This cute little cottage nestled between Washington Park and J.J. Byrne playground is the site of the 1776 Battle of Brooklyn, and now a colonial museum offering history lessons and community events. The adjacent playground has challenging climbing structures for older kids and an action-packed play area for younger kids, plus engaging water features that include a stream and spray jets. If you go on a Sunday, be sure to grab a snack at the Park Slope Farmers' Market next to it.

289 PIER 6 PLAYGROUND

Brooklyn Bridge
Park Greenway
Brooklyn Bridge
Park ④
*brooklynbridge
park.org/park/pier-6*

Pier 6 Playground is divided into four equally stupendous play areas: Waterlab is the home of the water elements designed to not only get your child wet but also teach them about the physics and dynamics of water. Slide Mountain is designed for children ages 5 to 12 and has several long and fast slides plus a climbing dome. Swing Valley Park includes Tarzan-style ropes and double-seaters. Finally, Sandbox Village is a large, enclosed sand area filled with ceramic and wooden structures. They all make for a lot of fun!

290 PROSPECT PARK ZOO

450 Flatbush
Avenue
Prospect Park ⑦
+1 718 399 7339
prospectparkzoo.com

The Prospect Park Zoo, a.k.a. the Brooklyn Zoo, has been around since 1890 and is located on the eastern side of Prospect Park. With its 12 acres (48.500 square meters), over 860 animals and over 176 species, it is the perfect place to entertain your little animal lovers. The whole interior can be comfortably walked in just a few hours. The sea lion show and feeding is a highlight, as is the Discovery Trail that takes you through a nicely curated collection of activities: tunnels that children can peer out of like prairie dogs, a spider web made of ropes to climb on, and dozens of ducks to feed. Also, don't miss the red pandas, an adorable river otter, emus, tufted deer, sprightly black-tailed prairie dogs, and dingoes.

Museums where kids have **F U N**

291 BROOKLYN CHILDREN'S MUSEUM

145 Brooklyn Avenue
Crown Heights ⑤
+1 718 735 4400
brooklynkids.org

The first children's museum in the world was this one. It was founded in 1899. The museum has something for kids of all ages. It teaches children about world cultures, history, science and nature in a fun way, and there is an area that is especially geared toward the youngest of youngsters. An expansion and renovation in 2008 made it the first green museum in New York City.

292 JEWISH CHILDREN'S MUSEUM

792 Eastern Parkway
Crown Heights ⑤
+1 718 467 0600
jcm.museum

This unique institution is a fun and educational environment for children and parents of all faiths and backgrounds. It is a place where one can explore Jewish history and heritage in a stimulating and interactive environment. The museum features multi-media spectacles, an art gallery, a game show studio, an audiovisual theater, a miniature golf course and a craft workshop.

293 NEW YORK AQUARIUM

602 Surf Avenue
Coney Island ®
+1 718 265 3474
nyaquarium.com

The New York Aquarium is the oldest continually operating aquarium in the USA. It is home to sharks, rays, sea otters, octopus, jellyfish and more. Catch the daily feeding of sea otters, walruses and penguins, admire the sea lion show at the Aquatheater, or see your favorite marine animals and meet some new ones along the way. Then cross the Coney Island boardwalk and go for a swim in the ocean!

294 WATERFRONT MUSEUM

290 Conover St
Red Hook ⑥
+1 718 624 4719
waterfront museum.org

David Sharps, a professional juggler and now president of the museum, saved Lehigh Valley Railroad Barge #79 more than 25 years ago and turned it into a floating museum. The barge is the only surviving all-wooden example of the Hudson River Railroad Barge that remains afloat. It now serves as a performance venue and an education center. There are collaborations with performing companies that include contradance, pirate shows, circus, dance, theatre, opera, and more.

295 **THE NEW YORK TRANSIT MUSEUM**

99 Schermer-
horn St
Downtown
Brooklyn ④
+1 718 694 1600
nytransitmuseum.org

Located in the decommissioned Court Street subway stop in downtown Brooklyn, this is one of the most charming and interesting museums in the city. The New York Transit Museum is dedicated, as its name indicates, to the city's transit system with beautifully conserved examples of subway and elevated cars, buses and trams from the 20th century, as well as archival objects and models, old photographs and reading material about how the city has been transformed by its transit system. The NY Times once aptly described it as 'a natural history museum of the city's public transportation'.

Cool **S K A T E P A R K S**
for the bigger kids

---

296 **COOPER SKATEPARK**

AT: COOPER PARK
**Sharon St and
Olive St
East Williams-
burg** ①
+1 212 639 9675
nycgovparks.org

Cooper is a personal favorite of many skaters in Brooklyn. On top of having all the traditional obstacles like rails and ledges, its many obstacles inspire you to get creative, such as a manual pad to rail, a rainbow rail over a euro gap, a slappy curb, and so on. All the obstacles are well built and smooth – particularly the quarter pipes, which are arguably the best in Brooklyn – and the local skaters are always warm and welcoming to everyone.

297 **GOLCONDA SKATEPARK (A.K.A. FAT KID)**

**Nassau St and
Gold St
Fort Greene** ④
+1 212 639 9675
nycgovparks.org

Known as Fat Kid by the locals, Golconda skatepark is a personal favorite. It features many different ledges of varying heights, incorporates good transition elements, and is set up in a way to promote creative skating through its layout. Additionally, Fat Kid is one of the bigger skateparks on this list, and almost never gets too crowded. The one drawback is that it does get a bit dirty because it is under a bridge. That said, it is still a wonderful park and worth a visit.

298 MARTINEZ PLAYGROUND SKATEPARK (A.K.A. BLUE PARK)

195 Graham Avenue
East Williamsburg ②
+1 212 639 9675
nycgovparks.org

Blue Park has in many ways become the cultural hub of Brooklyn skating. It is a small DIY skatepark with always changing obstacles. Located in Martinez Playground, adjacent to a high school, it has a wide range of creative obstacles that you won't find elsewhere. Additionally, you can move around many of the obstacles to your liking, allowing you to fully unleash your creativity. On top of this, Blue Park is often the center of many best trick competitions which has helped grow its 'cult' following. Being somewhat closely located to Cooper and McCarren, it is recommended you make a stop there, too.

299 MILLENNIUM SKATEPARK (A.K.A. OWL'S HEAD)

Colonial Road
Bay Ridge ⑧
+1 212 639 9675
nycgovparks.org

Owl's Head Skatepark, unlike the others on this list, is almost entirely transition. It features very little street skating elements such as ledges and rails, but this is entirely compensated for by the transition elements available. In the back of the park is a huge bowl that has depths ranging from 6 to 9 feet (1,9 to 2,75 meter), and towards the front there are more transition elements with hubbas and ledges meshed into the layout. Fair warning, the ground gets a bit rough in certain spots, but overall it is a great park, especially for transition skaters.

300 MCCARREN SKATEPARK

61 Bayard St
Williamsburg ①
+1 212 639 9675
nycgovparks.org

McCarren is known for its well-made obstacles and good flow. It features a euro gap, various round rails, a stair set, a set of hubbas, a pole jam, and a buttery smooth ledge. Additionally, it has a good number of transition elements that allow the park to flow really well. As McCarren Skatepark is closely located to Cooper Skatepark, it is highly recommended that you visit both when you are in the neighborhood as they are both regarded as some of the best skateparks in New York City.

SWEET SPOTS *for kids*

301 AMPLE HILLS – FIREBOAT HOUSE SCOOP SHOP

1 Water St
Brooklyn Bridge
Park ③
+1 718 852 0301
amplehills.com

Ample Hills considers this historical landmark at the foot of the Brooklyn Bridge on the Fulton Ferry Landing its flagship location. The Historic Fireboat House is where tourists (and sadly sometimes too many of them) and locals can munch through a wide variety of homemade ice creams and other frozen desserts, as well as a selection of non-dairy sorbets. It was here that Walt Whitman - American poet, journalist, and essayist – was inspired to write *Crossing Brooklyn Ferry*, one of his best-known and best-loved poems.

302 BROOKLYN FARMACY & SODA FOUNTAIN

513 Henry St
Carroll Gardens ⑥
+1 718 522 6260
*brooklynfarmacy
andsodafountain.com*

Brooklyn Farmacy & Soda Fountain is housed in a beautiful restored and renovated 1920s apothecary store that was once a booming neighborhood pharmacy. These days you come here with the entire family for sodas, sundaes, egg creams and comfort food. Sodas are all made with Farmacy's own syrups, ice cream are sourced from a small, all-natural producer, and there's a rotating menu of homemade baked goods.

303 LI-LAC CHOCOLATES

AT: INDUSTRY CITY
68 35th St, 1st Fl., Unit 18
Sunset Park ⑦
+1 212 924 2280
li-lacchocolates.com

When you visit the magic Li-Lac Chocolates' factory at Industry City in Sunset Park you are greeted by stacks of chocolates in nearly every shape imaginable, from high heels and lipstick to donkeys, dolphins, and everything in between. Li-Lac Chocolates was founded in 1923 by George Demetrious, a native of Greece, who emigrated to New York and opened his first shop in Greenwich Village, Manhattan. Now you can have a through-the-window view into their production facility and see the daily production in action.

304 VAN LEEUWEN

81 Bergen St
Boerum Hill ④
+1 347 763 2979
vanleeuwen icecream.com

Van Leeuwen is not Dutch. The company was founded by Australian Laura O'Neill and American brothers Ben and Pete Van Leeuwen, whose father is Dutch, and the ice cream is made in Greenpoint, Brooklyn. Only fresh milk, fresh cream, sugar and egg yolks are used, and the vegan ice cream is made with oat or cashew milk. You can find their scoop stores in Williamsburg, Prospect Heights, Greenpoint and Boerum Hill.

AKWAABA MANSION

SLEEP

Cozy **BED & BREAKFASTS**

305 **AKWAABA MANSION**

347 MacDonough St
Bedford-
Stuyvesant ⑤
+1 866 466 3855
akwaaba.com

Akwaaba is a beautifully restored 19th-century mansion in Bedford-Stuyvesant, owned by husband and wife team Glenn Pogue and Monique Greenwood. It is situated in a quiet tree-lined community alongside some of the most remarkable brownstones in the city, and only 15 minutes from Manhattan. Enjoy refreshments under the chestnut tree in the secluded garden or unwind in the Jacuzzi in your room. And make sure to pay a visit to the great Mama Fox restaurant around the corner on Stuyvesant Avenue.

306 **CARROLL GARDENS HOUSE**

284 President St
Carroll Gardens ⑥
+1 917 992 5052
carrollgardens
house.com

Carroll Gardens House consist of four clean, modern and spacious suites in two brownstones – one on President Street and one on Sackett Street – in the most charming neighborhood in Brooklyn. The family-friendly community has plenty of shops, restaurants and trees, and gives access to all of the features New York City has to offer with an abundance of Brooklyn charm.

Hotels with a
BREATHTAKING VIEW

---

307 1 HOTEL BROOKLYN BRIDGE

60 Furman St
Brooklyn Heights ③
+1 347 696 2500
1hotels.com/
brooklyn-bridge

The sustainable-conscious 1 Hotel leads the way with low-energy bulbs, five-minute shower timers, and locally sourced ingredients in its Neighbors cafe. The tranquil rooms are decorated in a soothing color palette and the furniture is naturally sourced. The pricier rooms have stunning Brooklyn Bridge and East River views, but if you can afford it, this is THE place to stay in Brooklyn.

308 THE BOX HOUSE HOTEL

77 Box St
Greenpoint ①
+1 718 383 3800
theboxhousehotel.com

The Box House must be one of the more authentic hotels in Brooklyn. This former factory has apartment-style rooms with vintage decoration or contemporary art, and large windows that flood the space with light. This is a hidden gem for those seeking breathing space and easy access to Manhattan. In addition, the waterfront is only a short walk from the hotel, and features stellar views.

309 THE WILLIAM VALE

111 N 12th St
Williamsburg ⓘ
+1 718 631 8400
thewilliamvale.com

This pillar – designed by Albo Liberis – on the Williamsburg skyline has views of Manhattan, Queens and Brooklyn from numerous vantage points. The rooms are hip and modern, with walls lined with eye-catching art from local artists and balconies with unobstructed views. It has an Italian restaurant, Leuca, the Westlight rooftop bar, and the city's longest outdoor pool. Throw in some film screenings and curated markets, and the William Vale defines luxury with a Brooklyn twist.

310 WYTHE HOTEL

80 Wythe Avenue
Williamsburg ⓘ
+1 718 460 8000
wythehotel.com

The lively rooftop Bar Blondeau with fantastic views, the wonderful Le Crocodile restaurant, and its cutting-edge industrial design make the Wythe on Williamsburg's waterfront a destination in itself. Rooms are roomy, with high ceilings, reclaimed wood furniture, and great amenities, handmade toiletries, heated concrete floors and cell phone-controlled surround sound. Noise, however, can be problematic especially if you are looking for a quiet place and want to relax. The lobby and the elevators can get crowded with non-guests on weekends, but they all add to the fun.

The William Vale

The COOL HOTELS
of Brooklyn

311 ACE HOTEL BROOKLYN

252 Schermer-
horn St
Boerum Hill ④
+1 718 313 3636
acehotel.com

In 2021, one of the hippest hotel chains opened its newest member of the family in Boerum Hill, on the edge of Downtown Brooklyn. Housed in a newly constructed brutalist building, Ace Hotel has 287 guest rooms, a cool bar called The Lobby, and a bakery counter named As You Are. Of course, everything has the distinctive artistic Ace vibe and it is reasonably priced.

312 THE WILLIAMS-BURG HOTEL

96 Wythe Avenue
Williamsburg ①
+1 718 362 8100
thewilliamsburg
hotel.com

This pet friendly hotel offers a number of perks including chauffeur-driven tuk-tuk rides, high tea service on weekends, and bike rentals. The space features plenty of exposed brick, locally made designer toiletries, a nightclub and seasonal outdoor pool, all with the most stunning unobstructed Manhattan views in one of Brooklyn's trendiest neighborhoods.

313 MCCARREN HOTEL & POOL

160 N 12th St
Williamsburg ①
+1 718 737 8548
mccarrenhotel.com

This stylish boutique hotel is popular with both Brooklynites and travelers because of the heated outdoor pool. Hotel guests and non-hotel guests can make reservations for the pool and enjoy the full-service bar and crafted cocktail menu. The vibe is great but it can become a very lively and a bit noisy get-together.

314 THE HOXTON

97 Wythe Avenue
Williamsburg ①
+1 718 215 7100
thehoxton.com

The Hoxton, a British boutique hotel, offers rooms in just two sizes, cozy or roomy. Both sizes are still rather small but big enough for a comfortable stay. Each room has notebooks with information and tips on the area, as well as a book collection curated by a local resident as part of the Hox-Friends program.

Where to sleep on a
SMALLER BUDGET

---

315 ALOFT NEW YORK BROOKLYN

216 Duffield St
Downtown
Brooklyn ④
+1 718 256 3833
marriott.com/hotels

This pet-friendly hotel is a short walk from lovely Fort Greene Park and close to the hip shops and restaurants of Cobble Hill. Aloft is all about trendy and exciting accommodation with an urban-influenced design, while the guest rooms provide all the essentials for budget travelers: an ultra-comfortable signature bed, a work desk, walk-in showers and bath amenities by Bliss Spa.

316 EVEN HOTEL BROOKLYN

46 Nevins St
Downtown
Brooklyn ④
+1 718 552 3800
ihg.com/evenhotels

This wellness hotel in Downtown Brooklyn near Nevin Station is within walking distance of the Brooklyn Bridge and Barclays Center. Each room has a fitness and work-out area, and you can cool off afterward in the spa-like showers. Complimentary Wi-Fi and flexible sit-or-stand workspaces are available should you need to work during your stay.

317 NY MOORE HOSTEL

179 Moore St
East Williams-
burg ②
+1 347 227 8634
nymoorehostel.com

The perfect place to meet other (world) travelers is located in a neighborhood with cool bars, music venues, galleries, cafes, restaurants and shops. Access to public transportation make other parts of Brooklyn and Manhattan easily accessible. The walls of this fun hostel display great street art and murals from artists from all over the world.

318 POD BROOKLYN

247 Metropolitan
Avenue
Williamsburg ①
+1 844 763 7666
thepodhotel.com/
pod-brooklyn

The Pod chain has a minimalist yet chic location in Brooklyn where bunk beds and efficient work desks make rooms look larger, and over-sized windows provide enough natural light. Perfect for the modern urban nomad. Travelers can relax on one of the four seasonal rooftop terraces and shared work spaces are great for connecting and collaborating.

PIER 2

WEEKEND ACTIVITIES ⚡

Best spots for **S P O R T S**

319 **GLEASON'S GYM**
130 Water St
Dumbo ③
+1 718 797 2872
gleasonsgym.com

It may look like an unassuming boxing club, but Gleason's Gym is the world's most famous and oldest boxing gym where the likes of Muhammad Ali, Mike Tyson, Jake LaMotta and countless other celebrities have trained. These days, anyone can get fit at Gleason's Gym – most of the members are regular New Yorkers learning how to box. The gym was founded in 1937 by Italian boxer Peter Gagliardi who changed his name to Bobby Gleason to appeal to the predominantly Irish New York fight crowd. The movie *Raging Bull* starring Robert De Niro was filmed here.

320 **THE CLIFFS AT DUMBO**
AT: MAIN STREET PARK
99 Plymouth St
Dumbo ③
+1 347 830 7625
dumbo.thecliffs climbing.com

This spacious facility located at Brooklyn Bridge Park's Main Street section, right under the Manhattan Bridge, holds the largest outdoor bouldering (bouldering means climbing without ropes!) area in North America. Experienced climbers and first-timers alike can explore its many tracks and challenges. Day passes are only 12 dollar, including shoes. This will be your new favorite place to climb, and during breaks you can take in the stunning views of Downtown Manhattan.

321 LEFRAK CENTER AT LAKESIDE PROSPECT PARK

171 East Drive
Prospect Park ⑦
+1 718 462 0010
lakeside
brooklyn.com

In winter, go for ice skating, figure skating, curling, hockey or broomball, and in summer there's roller skating, biking, boating and water play. LeFrak Center at Lakeside in Prospect Park has it all. The skate school offers classes for beginners and experienced skaters, and the hockey program includes lessons and league play for children and adults. The Bluestone Café has dining options as well as Brooklyn Brewery beers and an array of specialty wines.

322 PIER 2

150 Furman St
Brooklyn Bridge
Park ③
brooklynbridge
park.org/park/pier-2

Pier 2 in Brooklyn Bridge Park is packed with recreational courts and equipment including six basketball courts, ten handball courts, bocce courts, tetherball courts, 35 swings, chess tables, playgrounds, and picnic areas – not to mention free, seasonal kayaking programs. You can also strap on some skates and go for a spin at the Roller Rink. Pier 2 is open daily from 6 am to 8 pm.

323 RED HOOK RECREATION CENTER

155 Bay St
Red Hook ⑥
+1 718 722 3211
nycgovparks.org

The Sol Goldman Pool, an art moderne complex that opened in 1936 and one of NYC's biggest public swimming pools, was designed to accommodate more than 4462 people at a time. The building became a NYC landmark in 2008, and today the Olympic and wading pool are more popular, and necessary, than ever. Pool hours are from 11 am through 7 pm daily, with a break for pool cleaning between 3 pm and 4 pm. Only white T-shirts are allowed to be worn over your swimsuit as colored ones could mean you are in a gang!

Lovely **BIKE RIDES** in Brooklyn

324 **BROOKLYN SHORE PARKWAY BIKE TRAIL**

From Calvert Vaux Park to Owl's Head Park

Gravesend / Bay Ridge

This bike trail begins at Calvert Vaux Park and extends almost 7 miles (11,3 kilometers) north to Owl's Head Park. It is a scenic route with impressive views of Coney Island, the historical Fort Hamilton Army Base, the Verrazzano-Narrows Bridge, Staten Island's Fort Wadsworth and Battery Weed, the Statue of Liberty, and One World Trade Center. This fully paved trail has separate sections for cyclists and pedestrians, as well as several restrooms, benches, and parking areas along the way. It is heavily used by families, children, professional athletes, and everyone in between. The views and facilities make it worth the ride.

325 **JAMAICA BAY GREENWAY**

Loop around the area of Jamaica Bay

Jamaica Bay

This 19-mile (30-kilometer) cyclist and pedestrian loop in southern Brooklyn and Queens runs along a wildlife refuge that is the largest of its kind in the city. The Jamaica Bay Greenway brings you through an area full of all sorts of fauna and flora, as well as a few historical gems. There is so much to see and do on one of the longest bike rides in the city: go birdwatching at Jamaica Bay Wildlife Refuge, visit the abandoned ruins of Fort Tilden, or go for a swim at Jacob Riis Park.

326 BROOKLYN WATERFRONT GREENWAY

From Williamsburg to Brooklyn Bridge Park

brooklyn greenway.com

The Brooklyn Waterfront Greenway is a planned 26-mile (42-kilometer) route for pedestrians and cyclists along the Brooklyn Waterfront. At the time of writing, 18 miles (29 kilometers) of the route are finished. Start at Kent Avenue and N 7th Street in Williamsburg, ride south along Kent Avenue with views of the water and Manhattan to your right. Continue until Kent meets up with Flushing Avenue. Turn right on Flushing Avenue and continue until you hit Navy Street. Turn right on Navy Street and follow it as it curves to the left and turns into York Street, Dumbo. From there continue through Brooklyn Bridge Park. There is 6 miles (10 kilometers) to go to have the entire Greenway completed.

327 OCEAN PARKWAY COASTAL GREENWAY / JONES BEACH BIKE PATH

From Prospect Park to Coney Island

Ocean Parkway stretches over 5 miles (8 kilometers) connecting Prospect Park's southern boundary with the waterfront at Brighton Beach. The Parkway was built in the 19th century and became the home of the country's very first bike path of any historical significance. It was inspired by the grand boulevards of Europe and designed by Frederick Law Olmsted and Calvert Vaux (of Central Park and Prospect Park). The Ocean Parkway bike path continues to serve as the safest and most direct way for cyclists to make their way from central Brooklyn down to Coney Island.

328 PROSPECT PARK INNER LOOP

Prospect Park ⑦

Brooklyn's Prospect Park features a beautiful 3,35-mile (5,4-kilometer) loop that runs along the interior perimeter. The park is car-free during the weekend and has a dedicated bike lane at all times. The strong incline followed by a smooth downhill makes for the perfect place for cyclists of all levels. As for the bike, if you don't have one, head over to the LeFrak Center at Lakeside to rent one.

328 PROSPECT PARK INNER LOOP

Great **DAY TRIPS** *without a car*

329 **BOONTON, NEW JERSEY**

boonton.org

The Lakeland bus no. 46 takes you from Port Authority to Boonton center in about one hour. Once a thriving factory town, Boonton has gone through a revival in the past several decades, morphing into one of New Jersey's coolest destinations. For nature lovers the spectacular Boonton Falls are one of New Jersey's best kept secrets and are now part of the lovely Grace Lord Park. Boonton also offers plenty of options for art lovers with many art galleries on Main Street.

330 **GREENWICH, CONNECTICUT**

greenwichct.gov

Only one hour on the train from Grand Central Station, Greenwich, CT, is a sophisticated suburban community with large homes, beautiful shops and stylish restaurants. The Bruce Museum hosts a sizable collection of American impressionist art, as well as an impressive environmental science exhibit. Many bistros, cafes and restaurants featuring cuisines of many countries are to be found on the cosmopolitan Greenwich Avenue.

331 DIA:BEACON

3 Beekman St
Beacon NY 12508
+1 845 440 0100
diaart.org

Housed in a former Nabisco box-printing facility, Dia:Beacon is one of the largest exhibition spaces in the country. It is the perfect setting for Dia Foundation's permanent collection of art from the 1960s and 1970s to the present. Each of the artists shown have individual galleries fashioned specifically for their works, representing important late-20th-century art movements like abstract expressionism, minimalism, conceptual and pop art. Highlights include works by Andy Warhol, Dan Flavin, Louise Bourgeois, Donald Judd, Richard Serra and many more. To get there, take an 80-minute train ride from Grand Central and enjoy the stunning views of the Hudson River almost all the way.

332 HARRIMAN STATE PARK

Tuxedo NY 10975
myharriman.com

Take the NJ Transit in Penn Station to Tuxedo, NY, and from there a number of amazing trails start. This second-largest state park in New York has 200 miles (322 kilometers) of hiking trails, 3 beaches, and 32 lakes and reservoirs. In the fall, the entire place explodes with color as the leaves change. You can stay in 11 historic lean-tos (three-sided shelter built for the comfort of campers and hikers), excellent group campgrounds or at Beaver Pond Campground. Rent a kayak, canoe or rowboat at Baker Camp and explore the waters of Lake Sebago. There is also excellent fishing!

333 LONG BEACH, NEW YORK

longbeachny.gov

Long Beach is the only beach town that you can get to directly from Penn Station by the Long Island Rail Road within one hour. Make sure to get your beach pass along with your train ticket. The 2,25-mile (3,6 kilometer) boardwalk (built in 1914 with the help of some elephants) is wide, the sand of the beach is white and clean, and the ocean is beautiful. Don't miss the wonderful 1940's stucco Hollywood-style homes along its side streets.

334 PRINCETON, NEW JERSEY

princetonnj.gov

Princeton is one of the world's most famous college towns founded by Quakers near the banks of the Delaware River in 1675. To get there, take the New Jersey Transit in Penn Station and get off at Princeton Junction. There board the little one-car train called *the dinky* to Princeton Station. Visit the Princeton University Art Museum, take a stroll along the downtown Nassau Street, go shopping and dining in historic Palmer Square, or watch a show at the McCarter Theater Center.

335 RYE, NEW YORK

ryeny.gov

A trip to Rye takes about 45 minutes on the Metro-North train from Grand Central. This adorable town in Westchester is known for its iconic amusement park Playland that opened in 1928. Go for a ride on the famed Dragon Coaster, one of only about 100 wooden roller coasters still in operation in the USA. Rye's downtown has many cute shops, acres of lush forest and warm beaches. The Square House, an 18th-century inn on Purchase Street, is the headquarters for the Rye Historical Society and Museum.

336 SOUTH NORWALK, CONNECTICUT

visitsono.com

South Norwalk, or SoNo, has artistic flair, interesting shops and fine restaurants, all with a turn-of-the-century charm. The Metro-North train gets you there from Grand Central in just over an hour. This waterside village hosts the annual SoNo Arts Celebration in August, as well as the famed Oyster Festival in September. At the Maritime Aquarium you can interact with nearly 7000 animals. There's the Stepping Stones Museum for Children, and the Lockwood-Mathews Mansion Museum, one of the earliest and finest surviving Second Empire Style country houses ever built in the USA.

337 UNTERMYER PARK AND GARDENS

945 N Broadway
Yonkers NY 10701
+1 914 613 4502
untermyer gardens.org

The wealthy Samuel Untermyer, who was passionate about horticulture and gardening, purchased the 99-room mansion Greystone in 1899, and commissioned beaux-arts architect William Welles Bosworth to develop the estate. Untermyer, who provided public admittance to his gardens overlooking the Hudson River once a week until he died in 1940, left the estate to the City of Yonkers which opened it as a public park in 1946. Visit the Indo-Persian walled garden adorned with classical Greek structures, extensive mosaics, and figurative sculpture or the extensively planted garden that features an amphitheater, an annular array of Corinthian columns, and two cross-axial water channels converging in a central basin. Don't miss the romantic Temple of Love!

Experience the Brooklyn **P A R K S**

338 **BIRDWATCHING**

AT: PROSPECT PARK
**Prospect Park
Audubon Center
101 East Drive
Prospect Park** ⑦
+1 646 393 9031
prospectpark.org

Prospect Park is located along the Atlantic Flyway and therefore an ideal spot for birding. More than 250 species are spotted here each year, including migrating songbirds in spring and fall, and a large diversity of waterfowl and resident birds throughout the year. Early in migration, look for Yellow-bellied Sapsuckers, and, later in migration, look for Black-billed and Yellow-billed Cuckoos. The park also offers good birding during winter. The Christmas Bird Count, conducted by the Brooklyn Bird Club, has occasionally recorded more than 60 species in the park!

339 **PILOT**

**Pier 6,
Northwest edge
Brooklyn Bridge
Park** ④
pilotbrooklyn.com

If you ever dreamt of drinking champagne and slurping sustainably harvested oysters on one of America's most prized wooden schooners, then look no further. *Pilot* is a rare surviving Grand Banks style schooner that operates as an oyster bar and docks at Pier 6 in Brooklyn Bridge Park during the summer months.

340 CHERRY BLOSSOMS

AT: BROOKLYN
BOTANIC GARDEN
**990 Washington
Avenue
Prospect Park** ⑦
+1 718 623 7200
*bbg.org/collections/
cherries*

The monthlong cherry blossom season, called
Hanami, is a centuries-old Japanese tradition
of flower viewing. The blossoms are cherished
for their ephemeral nature and are thought to
represent the impermanence of life. The Brooklyn
Botanic Garden's Sakura Matsuri Festival is one
of the highlights of spring. It celebrates Japanese
culture with a rich program of events. It all
happens at Cherry Esplanade, a broad green lawn
bordered by avenues of flowering cherry and red
oak trees. The double-flowering Kanzan cherries
typically bloom at the end of April when thousands
of people swarm the Cherry Esplanade for pictures
beneath the twin rows of towering pink trees.

341 DRUMMER'S GROVE

**Parkside and
Ocean Avenues
entrance
Prospect Park** ⑦
+1 718 965 8951
prospectpark.org

The Congo Square Drummers started gathering
in Prospect Park informally in 1968 for a drum
circle at the southeastern corner of the park.
Over the years, the drum circle grew, and the
area became a destination for musicians, dancers,
vendors and craftsmen. In 1997, the Prospect Park
Alliance added seating to the area and named
it Drummer's Grove. It continues to be a place
where anyone can stop by every Sunday, from
April through October, 2 pm to dusk to play,
dance, or simply enjoy the music.

342 JANE'S CAROUSEL

AT: EMPIRE FULTON
FERRY PARK
Old Dock St
Dumbo ③
+1 718 222 2502
janescarousel.com

Jane's Carousel is a completely restored historic carousel made in 1922 by the Philadelphia Toboggan Company for the Idora Park amusement park in Youngstown, Ohio. It was bought by Dumbo developers Jane and David Walentas, and moved from Ohio in 1984. Jane Walentas painstakingly restored the merry-go-round over the years, and it was installed on the Dumbo waterfront in 2011. Its 48 horses prance near the East River year-round, protected from the elements by a jewel-box structure designed by Pritzker Prize-winning French architect Jean Nouvel. Rides are just 2 dollar.

343 JOURNEY TO THE STARS

Pier 1 Promenade
Brooklyn Bridge
Park ③
+1 718 222 9939
brooklynbridge
park.org

On select Friday nights in August and September, members of the Amateur Astronomers Association of New York set up hi-powered telescopes to see the stars, planets and the moon from Brooklyn Bridge Park. Join the astronomers at the Pier 1 Promenade as they guide your eyes across the sky and the wonders of astronomy are revealed. The event is free and open to the public, but it's first come, first served.

RED HOOK

RANDOM FACTS
& URBAN DETAILS 🔍

344 4TH OF JULY FIREWORKS
Various spots
macys.com/social/fireworks

The 4th of July Fireworks have been happening for more than 40 years and are one of the largest celebrations in the nation. Usually they are ignited from barges in the East River near the Brooklyn Bridge, but do check ahead of time. Watch from a blanket in Brooklyn Bridge Park or grab a bench on the Brooklyn Heights Promenade for views along the Brooklyn waterfront. You can also catch a spot further north in Domino Park. But it doesn't matter where you go, just be sure to arrive several hours early to secure your spot; fireworks are set to start at approximately 9.20 pm.

345 MERMAID PARADE
Coney Island
coneyisland.com

This fun NYC attraction takes place on the Saturday closest to the summer solstice. Thousands of onlookers gather in Coney Island to watch King Neptune and Queen Mermaid lead a procession of half-naked mermaids, mermen and other creatures covered in glitter and scales. The parade begins at Surf Avenue and W 21st Street, travels along Surf Avenue and the Boardwalk before ending at Steeplechase Plaza. For the best chance of getting a good spot, show up by 11 am.

346 NYC MARATHON

Various spots
nyrr.org/
tcsnycmarathon

In 1970, the first NYC Marathon took place
entirely within Central Park with 127 entrants,
55 finishers and a 1-dollar entry fee. The route now
winds through all five boroughs and is the largest
marathon in the world. Brooklyn is the flattest (and
thus the fastest) borough on the course. The only
two years the race was cancelled was in 2012, when
the city was recovering from Hurricane Sandy,
and in 2020 due to the pandemic. Participating in
the race depends on a lottery application, and the
winner gets 100.000 dollar.

347 WEST INDIAN DAY PARADE

Crown Heights
wiadcacarnival.org

The West Indian Day Parade or Labor Day Parade
celebrates Caribbean culture and takes place on the
first Monday in September. This annual celebration
started in Harlem in the 1930s and moved to Crown
Heights in 1969. It attracts more than a million
spectators and participants from around the world.
Plenty of colorful costumes, fabulous masks, steel
bands, reggae, and food from every Caribbean
nation along Eastern Parkway.

What's in a **NAME**

────────────

348 DUMBO

Originally known as Fulton Landing, the area was renamed Dumbo by residents and artist loft tenants in the late 1970s. The name is an acronym for the area's location Down Under the Manhattan Bridge Overpass. It was meant to be an uncool, anti-marketing name to protect the neighborhood from developers and to alarm real estate brokers in fear of gentrification. The opposite happened, it is now one of Brooklyn's most trendy and expensive neighborhoods. Fun fact: the alternative name they came up with was DANYA: District Around the Navy Yard Annex, but DUMBO won.

349 RED HOOK AND BAY RIDGE

The village of *Roode Hoek* (Dutch for Red Corner) was settled by Dutch colonists of New Amsterdam in 1636. Red Hook got its name because of the red soil and the point of land. Further south was Yellow Hook, which had also a peninsular shape but with yellow soil. In 1853, the name's negative connotation with Yellow Fever caused residents to rename the area. They picked Bay Ridge, for the glacial ridge that separates the land from New York Bay.

350 SHEEPSHEAD BAY

This neighborhood took its name from an eponymous hotel that was established here in 1844. The hotel was named after the sheepshead fish (Archosargus probatocephalus), an edible saltwater fish with sheep-like teeth that populated the namesake bay off the eastern coast of Coney Island before it mysteriously vanished.

351 AVENUES FROM H TO Z
Various locations

The story goes that in 1910 a Mr Brown, a member of the Flatbush Board of Trade, felt the names in Ditmas Park and surroundings were too boring and lacked a distinctive flavor compared with the rest of early Brooklyn. He wanted to give the avenues from H to Z more colorful representations from Native American, Dutch and English sources. Like Avenue H – Hiawatha Avenue, Avenue N – Nottingham Road, Avenue W – Wilhelmina Road. Unfortunately, the other members of the board found this unimportant and suggested that the simple letter names were 'good enough to please the majority of taxpayers'.

352 VINEGAR HILL

This small, cobblestoned neighborhood on the East River waterfront between Dumbo and the Brooklyn Navy Yard was named after the 1798 Battle of Vinegar Hill in Ireland where Irish rebels were crushed by the English. With the name Vinegar Hill, they tried to entice the wave of Irish immigrants to settle in that area. And indeed, the neighborhood came to be populated by Irish dockworkers, many holding jobs at the Navy Yard, which is why the area became locally known as Irish Town.

CAPTIVATING NOVELS
about Brooklyn

---

353 **A TREE GROWS IN BROOKLYN**
BY BETTY SMITH

Williamsburg

A Tree Grows in Brooklyn is a classic novel written in 1943 by Brooklyn-born Betty Smith. Largely autobiographical and published in 1943, the novel portrays Williamsburg at the beginning of the 20th century as a settling place for immigrants coming through Ellis Island. It references Italian, Irish and Jewish communities and describes the tough living conditions of tenement housing.

354 **BROOKLYN**
BY COLM TÓIBÍN

Downtown Brooklyn

In this 2009 trans-Atlantic coming-of-age story by Irish writer Colm Tóibín, the main character moves from her tiny Irish village to Brooklyn. Due to a family crisis back home, the Irish immigrant has to make a choice between the past and the future, the old world and the new world, in Brooklyn in the early 1950s.

355 **THE BROOKLYN FOLLIES**
BY PAUL AUSTER

Park Slope

Paul Auster lives with his wife, the writer Siri Hustvedt, in beautiful Park Slope near Prospect Park. The *Brooklyn Follies* is a love letter to Auster's neighborhood, and it's through imagination that the place really comes alive. It is a novel striving for a true sense of community.

356 DECODED
BY JAY-Z
Bedford-
Stuyvesant

Decoded (2010) is the autobiography and memoir of rapper Jay-Z, a.k.a. Shawn Carter, who grew up in Brooklyn's drug-infested Marcy housing projects in Bedford-Stuyvesant. Jay-Z tells the story of his start in the industry, his most important influences, and his rise from poverty. Growing up in a rough neighborhood in Brooklyn shaped his worldview and his work in the music industry.

357 LAST EXIT TO BROOKLYN
BY HUBERT SELBY JR.
Sunset Park /
Bay Ridge

The first novel by Brooklyn-born Hubert Selby Jr., *Last Exit to Brooklyn*, was published in 1964. This cult classic novel was made into a movie in 1989 and was set almost entirely in what is now considered Sunset Park. The location is widely misreported as Red Hook. There are drug addicts, mobsters, prostitutes and thieves brawling in the back alleys of Brooklyn. This explosive best-seller has come to be regarded as a classic of modern American writing.

358 TROPIC OF CAPRICORN
BY HENRY MILLER
Williamsburg

According to the *New Yorker*, Henry Miller energetically hated New York calling it 'that old shithole, New York, where I was born' late in life. He was born in Williamsburg and later spent time in Bushwick, Park Slope and Brooklyn Heights. *Tropic of Capricorn*, published in 1939, is famous for its frank portrayal of life in Brooklyn's ethnic neighborhoods, and Miller's outrageous sexual exploits. This semi-autobiographical novel was banned in America for almost thirty years but is now considered a cornerstone of modern literature.

INDEX

COLOPHON

EDITING *and* COMPOSING — Katelijne De Backer — kadebeconsulting.com

GRAPHIC DESIGN — Joke Gossé and doublebill.design

PHOTOGRAPHY — Gabriel Flores — gabrielrobertflores.com

COVER IMAGE — Nathan's Famous (secret 32)

The addresses in this book have been selected after thorough independent
research by the author, in collaboration with Luster Publishing. The selection
is solely based on personal evaluation of the business by the author. Nothing
in this book was published in exchange for payment or benefits of any kind.

D/2022/12.005/7
ISBN 978 94 6058 3001
NUR 510, 513

© 2022 Luster Publishing, Antwerp
First edition, February 2022
lusterpublishing.com — THE500HIDDENSECRETS.COM
info@lusterpublishing.com

Printed in Italy by Printer Trento.